LUTHER'S FIRST FRONT

The Eucharist as Sacrifice

Robert C. Croken, S.J.

University of Ottawa Press
Ottawa • London • Paris

©University of Ottawa Press, 1990
ISBN 0-7766-0300-0
Printed and bound in Canada

Canadian Cataloguing in Publication Data

Croken, Robert C., 1933-
Luther's first front: the Eucharist as sacrifice

Includes bibliographical references.
ISBN 0-7766-0300-0

1. Luther, Martin, 1483-1546 — Views on Lord's
Supper.   2. Lord's Supper — Lutheran Church.
3. Lord's Supper — Catholic Church.   4. Lutheran
Church — Doctrines.   5. Catholic Church — Doctrines.
I. Title.

BV823.C76 1990   234'.163   C90-090407-0

UNIVERSITÉ UNIVERSITY
D'OTTAWA   OF OTTAWA

Imprimi Potest: William M. Addley, S.J.
March 13, 1990

This book has been published with the help of a grant from the Canadian Federation for the
Humanities, using funds provided by the Social Sciences and Humanities Research Council
of Canada.

Design: Judith Gregory

Cover: Adrien Daveau (French)
Chalice (Silver) 1691–1698
©The National Gallery of Canada, Ottawa

CONTENTS

INTRODUCTION

ne significant advantage of the contemporary ecumenical dialogue is that it occasions serious historical investigation of areas of doctrine that have been disputed and often misunderstood by Christian denominations since the time of the Reformation. Sincere dialogue by participants raises questions about the concrete historical circumstances that gave rise to such differences and how these have been passed on through generations. The same sincere dialogue must often acknowledge that, although research has removed much misunderstanding and bias, full agreement is not yet attained.

Such an area of disputed doctrine is the sacrificial dimension of the Eucharist. Although this is a subject of considerable controversy within the major Christian denominations, this study will limit its investigation to the genesis of the issue between the Roman Catholic and Lutheran traditions. It will undertake a systematic analysis of this dimension of the Eucharist in the writings of Martin Luther in the context of his break with Rome in order to contribute some further understanding to the continuing Lutheran–Roman Catholic dialogue.

Both in North America and in Europe, ecumenical discussions by Lutherans and Roman Catholics have explored many important areas of the Christian faith. Since 1965 in the United States, theologians have met periodically as official representatives of both traditions and, to date, their discussions have resulted in seven publications, beginning with the Nicene Creed and proceeding to justification by faith. Two of these publications have dealt with the Eucharist: *The Eucharist as*

Sacrifice and *Eucharist and Ministry.*[1] Both works contain position papers by competent theologians and a joint statement honestly setting forth points of agreement and points that demand further study and clarification before mutual acceptance is possible. Papers and discussions of the Lutheran–Roman Catholic dialogue on the Eucharist in Germany, 1976–1982, accompanied by a summary statement, have been edited by Karl Lehmann and Edmund Schlink in *Das Opfer Jesu Christi und seine Gegenwart in der Kirche: Klärungen zum Opfercharakter des Herrenmahles* (Freiburg i. Br., 1983).

On the international level, the Vatican Secretariat for Christian Unity and the Lutheran World Federation issued the "Catholic–Lutheran Agreed Statement on the Eucharist" in 1978.[2] Incorporating the fruit of ecumenical discussions by these world bodies and including the research of European as well as North American theologians, this document presents a comprehensive and positive "joint witness" on the meaning of the Eucharist. The Eucharist as sacrifice is treated in Part II under "Common Tasks," indicating again an aspect of the Eucharist on which, while a much greater measure of understanding has been reached, full agreement is not yet possible. These ecumenical statements, as well as some recent texts of the Faith and Order Commission of the World Council of Churches, will be taken up in more detail in the concluding chapter of this study.

It is clear, then, that the Eucharist occupies an important place in contemporary ecumenical discussions, and that its sacrificial dimension remains an area of incomplete agreement in these discussions. This ought not to be surprising because, being a contentious issue at the time of the Reformation, it has remained a divisive topic over the centuries, particularly between Roman Catholic and Protestant denominations; hence, it has also remained a neglected area of research until the ecumenical dialogue of this century motivated a re-examination of the meaning of the Eucharist as sacrifice.

As shall be seen, it was this aspect of the Eucharist that Luther first vigorously opposed in his controversy with Rome. It constituted one of his principal objections to traditional eucharistic doctrine during

[1] *Lutherans and Catholics in Dialogue* III & IV. Joint publications of the U.S.A. National Committee of the Lutheran World Federation and the Bishops' Commission for Ecumenical Affairs, Washington, 1967 and 1970 respectively.
[2] An English translation may be found in *Origins* VIII (January 1979), 466–78.

what Dr. Carl Wisløff has called the "First Front" against the papists.[3] In 1526, with the publication of his *Sermon von dem Sakrament des Leibes und Blutes Christi, wider die Schwarmgeister*, Luther engaged in a "Second Front" of controversy, concerning the mode of the presence of Christ in the Eucharist, initially with the Enthusiasts and later with Zwingli and Calvin.[4] It has been the controversial literature of this second phase that, until recently, has dominated research into Luther's understanding of the Eucharist.[5]

This study will focus on what absorbed Luther during the "First Front" of his career: his rejection of the Eucharist as a sacrifice and a good work.[6] It will begin with an analysis of the principal works of the Luther *corpus* in which he deals with this subject. While his fundamental positions were well established in his writings before 1526, he continued to object to the sacrificial dimension of the Eucharist until the end of his life; consequently, some of his later works will also be examined. Following this analysis of what Luther said, it will be possible, in Part II, to formulate positively the main elements of his theology of the Eucharist and to appreciate how this understanding was incompatible with that of the Eucharist as sacrifice. It will then be instructive, from a Roman Catholic viewpoint, to explore how Luther's position on the Eucharist implied differences with respect to other related doctrines, such as the nature of the atonement and the mediation of grace. Points of doctrinal agreement present even in the sixteenth century will also be examined and, in conclusion, the bases for agreement offered by contemporary research and the above-mentioned

---

[3] Carl F. Wisløff, *The Gift of Communion*, trans. Joseph M. Shaw (Minneapolis, 1964), p. 2; his terminology has been used in the title of this study.

[4] Paul Althaus, *The Theology of Martin Luther*, trans. Robert C. Schultz (Philadelphia, 1966), pp. 375–76, makes a similar distinction in Luther's theology of the Eucharist, although he dates the shift in 1524. Helmut Feld, *Das Verständnis des Abendmahls* (Darmstadt, 1976), pp. 110–15, agrees with Althaus' two-stage division of Luther's writings on the Eucharist.

[5] Cf., for example, Reinhold Seeberg's *Lehrbuch der Dogmengeschichte* IV, 1 (5th ed., Graz, 1953). Pages 405–407 summarize Luther's treatment of the Eucharist as a sacrifice and a good work, while a separate chapter (pp. 433–78) is devoted to Luther's eucharistic doctrine vis-à-vis that of Zwingli.

[6] Jared Wicks, in the forefront of contemporary Catholic research on Luther, regards this aspect of the eucharistic controversy as one of the three central points of doctrine in which Luther was at variance with Catholic tradition. See *Luther and His Spiritual Legacy* (Wilmington, Del., 1983), pp. 29–30.

ecumenical statements will be reviewed, and an area of further research in which fuller agreement might be achieved on this issue will be suggested. In this way, it is hoped that the present study will contribute to the growing body of literature on this important aspect of eucharistic doctrine[7] and to the continuing ecumenical dialogue, particularly between Lutherans and Roman Catholics.

---

[7]   Much of the research so far has come from German theologians, both Lutheran and Catholic, most notably: Erwin Iserloh, *Der Kampf um die Messe in den ersten Jahren der Auseinandersetzung mit Luther* (Münster, 1952), and, with Peter Meinhold, *Abendmahl und Opfer* (Stuttgart, 1966); Hans Bernhard Meyer, *Luther und die Messe* (Paderborn, 1965); Wilhelm Averbeck, *Der Opfercharakter des Abendmahls in der neueren evangelischen Theologie* (Paderborn, 1966); Ferdinand Pratzner, *Messe und Kreuzesopfer. Die Krise der sakramentalen Idee bei Luther und in der mittelalterlichen Scholastik* (Wien, 1970); Frido Mann, *Das Abendmahl beim jungen Luther* (Munich, 1971); and Wolfgang Schwab, *Entwicklung und Gestalt der Sakramententheologie bei Martin Luther* (Frankfurt, 1977). In addition to the Norwegian theologian, Carl Wisløff (cf. note 3), whose *Nattverd og Messe—en studie i Luthers teologi* was also translated into German as *Abendmahl und Messe* (Berlin/Hamburg, 1969), mention should be made of the work of Hungarian theologian, Vilmos Vajta, whose *Die Theologie des Gottesdienstes bei Luther* (Göttingen, 1954) was translated into English by U. S. Leupold as *Luther on Worship* (Philadelphia, 1958).

PART I
Luther's Writings on the Eucharist

CHAPTER I
1517–1520

artin Luther was born at Eisleben on November 10, 1483, to Hans and Margarethe Luther.[1] For his early schooling, he went to nearby Magdeburg and Eisenach. In 1501, he matriculated in the Faculty of Arts at the University of Erfurt where he subsequently obtained his bachelor's degree in 1505. At the time, the Augustinian Friars were affiliated with the university and, in July of that same year, Luther decided under unusual circumstances to enter their Order. Actually, they were a branch of the Augustinians known under the official title of "Reformed Congregation of the Eremitical Order of St. Augustine."[2] Two years later, in April 1507, Luther was ordained a priest and on May 2 celebrated his first Mass. For the next five years, he continued his studies in theology while teaching at the University of Wittenberg, lecturing on the Psalms, the Epistles to the Romans and Hebrews, and publishing his lectures.[3]

---

[1] Ian Siggins, in his little book *Luther and His Mother* (Philadelphia, 1981), has provided interesting material on Luther's family background, establishing that his mother was Margarethe Lindemann, not Margarethe Ziegler.

[2] In 1473, Andreas Proles had carried through a reform of the Augustinian Order and the House of Erfurt was numbered among those Observant Houses which accepted a strict interpretation of their rule, with Proles as Vicar-General. Cf. Gordon Rupp, *Luther's Progress to the Diet of Worms* (New York, 1964), p. 15.

[3] Biographical data on Luther's life may be found in some detail in Joseph Lortz, *The Reformation in Germany* I, trans. Ronald Walls (New York, 1968), pp. 175ff.; in Roland Bainton's popular *Here I Stand: A Life of Martin Luther* (New York, 1950); and in more recent biographies, e.g., James Atkinson, *Martin Luther and the Birth of Protestantism* (2nd ed., Atlanta, Ga., 1981); John M. Todd, *Luther: A Life* (New York, 1982); H. G. Haile, *Luther: An Experiment in Biography* (New York, 1980); Martin

Since at this early period of his career Luther was a friar in good standing, it is not surprising that he shows little opposition to the notion of eucharistic sacrifice in his earliest publications. To the extent that he discusses the subject at all in his *Dictata super Psalterium*, it is of secondary importance.[4] The true Christian sacrifice is the sacrifice of ourselves. This self-oblation aspect is further associated with the sacrifice of the Eucharist in his *Divi Pauli apostoli ad Romanos Epistola*, but the validity of the Mass as sacrifice itself is not challenged.[5] The first evidence of serious questioning appears in his *Commentariolus in epistolam divi Pauli Apostoli ad Hebraeos*.

Luther's commentary on Hebrews is based on his lectures, delivered at Wittenberg University in the period from April 1517 to March 1518. It was during this same period that his celebrated controversy with Rome on the question of indulgences arose. Disturbed by the exaggerated, even erroneous, preaching of a Dominican friar, Johann Tetzel (c. 1465–1519), whose influence may have reached some of the parishioners of the City Church at Wittenberg where Luther preached, he drew up a series of ninety-five theses concerning the doctrine and practice of indulgences. On the eve of the Feast of All Saints, October 31, 1517, Luther dispatched these theses to Albert of Brandenburg, Archbishop of Mainz (1490–1545).[6] In an accompanying letter, he indicated that he was mainly concerned with the erroneous ideas about indulgences being preached—for example, that the faithful, by purchasing letters of pardon, could secure their salvation and that "as soon as the coin in the coffer rings, / the soul from purgatory springs."[7] But

---

Brecht, *Martin Luther*: Bd. 1 *Sein Weg zur Reformation, 1483–1521* (Stuttgart, 1981); Bd. 2 *Ordnung und Abgrenzung der Reformation, 1521–1532* (1986); Bd. 3 *Die Erhaltung der Kirche, 1532–1546* (1987). Bd. 1 has been translated by James L. Schaaf, *Martin Luther: His Road to Reformation, 1483–1521* (Philadelphia, 1985).

4   This is the opinion of Wisløff, *The Gift of Communion*, p. 12, and he is supported here by such a stern Catholic critic of Luther as Hartmann Grisar, *Luther* I (London, 1913), p. 74, who sees no denial of Catholic doctrine in Luther's commentary on the Psalms. Cf. also Mann, *Das Abendmahl beim jungen Luther*, pp. 129–30.

5   Wisløff, *The Gift of Communion*, pp. 12–13.

6   Whether or not Luther dramatically nailed the theses to the door of the Castle Church was a point much discussed by German scholars in the 1960s. Cf. references in Mark U. Edwards, Jr., "Martin Luther," in Steven Ozment, ed., *Reformation Europe: A Guide to Research* (St. Louis, 1982), p. 67, n. 29. I favour the position established by Erwin Iserloh, *Luther zwischen Reform und Reformation. Der Thesenanschlag fand nicht statt* (3rd ed., Münster, 1968).

7   Bainton, *Here I Stand*, p. 60.

the tenor of some of the theses was challenged by the Dominican theologian, Sylvester Prierias (1456–1523), Master of the Sacred Palace, and later by Cardinal Cajetan (1463–1534), the papal representative, appointed to mediate the widening conflict.[8] The publication of the theses on indulgences proved to be the first of a series of events that led Luther into open conflict with the authority of the Roman Church and, ultimately, to his definitive excommunication in January 1521.[9] For present purposes it is sufficient to observe that his initial criticism of the external means of salvation without the accompanying condition of faith is coincident with his lectures on Hebrews.

Evidence of such criticism appears, then, in his published commentary on Hebrews. In the context of the sacrifices of the Old Testament and their efficacy (Heb. 9:9), Luther observes that they were powerless to purify the conscience of the worshipper; only if they were accompanied by faith and love could they effect this. Here, Luther sees a continuity between the sacrifices of the Old Testament and the sacraments of the New Testament: for him, it is not the sacraments themselves but faith in the sacraments that makes one righteous.[10] Con-

---

[8] On Prierias, cf. Carter Lindberg, "Prierias and His Significance for Luther's Development," *The Sixteenth Century Journal* III (October 1972), 45–64; on Cajetan, cf. the introductory biographical essay by Jared Wicks in *Cajetan Responds: A Reader in Reformation Controversy* (Washington, D.C., 1978), pp. 3–46, and his article, "Fides sacramenti—Fides specialis: Luther's Development in 1518," *Gregorianum* LXV (Fasc. #1, 1984), 53–87; on Luther's meeting with Cajetan at Augsburg, cf. Otto Hermann Pesch, *Hinführung zu Luther* (Mainz, 1982), pp. 103–15 and, again, Jared Wicks, *Cajetan und die Anfänge der Reformation* (Münster, 1983), pp. 43–112.

[9] The events of these crucial years for Luther have been ably treated by Robert E. McNally, "The Ninety-Five Theses of Martin Luther: 1517–1967," *Theological Studies* XXVIII (September 1967), 439–80; Jared Wicks, *Man Yearning for Grace* (Washington, 1968), pp. 216–64; DeLamar Jensen, *Confrontation at Worms* (Provo, Ut., 1973); Daniel Olivier, *The Trial of Luther*, trans. John Tonkin (London, 1978); Scott H. Hendrix, *Luther and the Papacy: Stages in a Reformation Conflict* (Philadelphia, 1981); Jared Wicks, "Roman Reactions to Luther: The First Year (1518)," *Catholic Historical Review* LIX (October 1983), 521–62; and, less satisfactorily, James Atkinson, *The Trial of Luther* (New York, 1971).

[10] *D. Martin Luthers Werke*, 57, 206; *LW* 29, 207. Subsequent references to this official Weimar edition of Luther's writings will be indicated as *WA*, followed by the volume number in Arabic numerals and the page reference. Where a translation of the reference is available in the American edition of *Luther's Works*, eds. Jaroslav Pelikan and Helmut T. Lehmann (St. Louis & Philadelphia, 1955–), this will be included with the abbreviation *LW*. Since such references will be numerous, they will be included within brackets in the text.

science, purified and made calm through faith, experiences joy in the remission of sin and no longer dreads punishments. No law, no works contribute to this purity of conscience—only faith by which we believe that the blood of Christ has been shed for our sins (*WA* 57, 207–208; *LW* 29, 207).

Commenting on the text of Hebrews 9:17, "For a will takes effect only at death . . . ,"[11] Luther stresses the interpretation of Christ's testament as his last will. Christ made a will, so to speak, and left us immeasurable blessings: the remission of sins and eternal life. This interpretation applies even to "testament" in the words of institution (Matt. 26:28): "With these most delightful words He bequeaths to us, not the riches or the glory of the world but once and for all absolutely all blessings, that is . . . the remission of sins and possession of the future kingdom" (*WA* 57, 212; *LW* 29, 213). "Testament," with this meaning, was to become an important theological concept for Luther in formulating his theology of the Eucharist.[12]

The Epistle to the Hebrews emphasizes the oneness and uniqueness of the expiatory sacrifice of Christ, a sacrifice offered once for all time. Yet, in the Christian tradition, as it was known to Luther, Christ is said to be offered for us every day in the Eucharist. As a solution to this important difficulty, Luther makes a distinction between "oblatio" and "memoria oblationis," in which what we offer daily is said to be not so much a sacrifice as a remembrance of that sacrifice. This is the force of Christ's command: "Do this in remembrance of me" (Lk. 22:19). Consequently, Christ cannot be said to suffer by reason of the fact that he is remembered to have suffered (*WA* 57, 217–18; *LW* 29, 219–20).

In dealing further with this very difficulty, Luther introduced a second important distinction between the sacrifice of Christ and the sacrifice of the Church:

---

[11]   All scriptural references, unless otherwise indicated, will be from the Revised Standard Version.

[12]   Kenneth Hagen, in his *A Theology of Testament in the Young Luther. The Lectures on Hebrews* (Leiden, 1974), has undertaken a careful study of the notion of testament in Luther's earlier writings to 1517, against the background of Augustine and the medieval exegesis of Hebrews. In this wider meaning of testament, Hagen interprets Luther as locating the element of continuity in the testament itself: in the context of the Old and New Testaments, it is better to speak of one testament of God, received in two ways, as law and as spirit. Cf. especially pp. 68–70; and for testament as applied to the Eucharist, pp. 108–14.

> The sacrifice of the New Testament is perfect and has ceased completely so far as the Head of the church, who is Christ, is concerned; but the spiritual sacrifice of His body, which is the church, is offered from day to day, when the church dies constantly with Christ and celebrates the mystical Passover, namely, when it slays lusts and passes over from this world to future glory (WA 57, 218; LW 29, 220).

Neither of these distinctions is developed by Luther at this stage of the formulation of his doctrine; they are made simply in order to underline his principal statement, that the sacrifice of Christ is a past, unrepeatable event. At the same time, it is curious to observe that he does not make use of several passages of Hebrews which would seem to reinforce this kind of interpretation, for example Heb. 7:27: "He [Christ] has no need, like those high priests, to offer sacrifice daily, first for his own sins and then for those of the people; he did this once for all when he offered up himself."[13] It is less surprising that certain other passages (for example, Heb. 8:1–3, describing Christ's high priestly function in the heavenly sanctuary), which might argue for some continuity of Christ's sacrifice, are without comment. This evidence would simply indicate that, at this early stage of Luther's doctrinal development, the continuity of the sacrifice of Christ in the Eucharist is not yet a point of contention for him and therefore he is not in search of arguments for his position.

In 1519, Luther wrote three sermons on the sacraments. The first deals with penance,[14] the second with baptism,[15] and the third with the Eucharist, entitled *Ein Sermon von dem hochwürdigen Sakrament des heiligen wahren Leichnams Christi und von den Brüderschaften*. This treatise, Luther's first extensive statement on the Lord's Supper, is principally a devotional work, containing a positive exposition of the meaning of Holy Communion; it does not, however, explicitly raise the theological issues of either the sacrifice of the Mass or the Real Presence (LW 35, 47). Nevertheless, like his commentary on Hebrews, it contains certain emphases that become significant later in Luther's more controversial works.

---

[13]   Similar passages are passed over without comment: 10:10; 10:12–14; 10:18.
[14]   *Ein Sermon von dem Sakrament der Busse.*
[15]   *Ein Sermon von dem heiligen hochwürdigen Sakrament der Taufe.*

In his conception of the sacraments in general, it is noteworthy that Luther, at least at this stage of development, almost equates "sacrament" with external sign. Bread and wine constitute the sacrament or external sign of the Eucharist, just as water is the sign of baptism. The sign indicates the use that ought to be made of the sacrament: water in baptism is used by immersion or pouring; bread and wine in the Eucharist are used in eating and drinking (WA 2, 742; LW 35, 49). The sacrament in turn indicates its significance and effect. Eating bread and drinking wine in the Eucharist signify the complete and undivided fellowship of the saints (WA 2, 742–43; LW 35, 50). Luther uses the analogy of a city as a community to explain the union of all the saints with one another and with Christ:

> Hence it is that Christ and all the saints are one spiritual body, just as the inhabitants of a city are one community and body, each citizen being a member of the other and of the entire city. All the saints, therefore, are members of Christ and of the Church, which is a spiritual and eternal city of God (WA 2, 743; LW 35, 51).

On a deeper level, this fellowship results from the fact that all the spiritual possessions of Christ and his saints are shared with, and become the common property of, the one who receives this sacrament (WA 2, 743; LW 35, 51). This is simply an accurate formulation of the traditional doctrine of the communion of saints!

According to the rite and manner in which the Eucharist was celebrated in 1519, Luther saw little that expressed and fostered such fellowship. Thus, according to him, the principal meaning of the sacrament was not explained by the preachers; instead, the people were being treated to humanly devised tales of works of satisfaction that they must perform to live rightly (WA 2, 747; LW 35, 56–57). Many Masses were celebrated and little attention was given to celebrating or attending them worthily. The important matter seemed to be the ritual celebration of Masses: "There are many who . . . rely upon the fact that the mass or the sacrament is, as they say, *opus gratum opere operato*, that is, a work which of itself pleases God, even though they who perform it do not please him" (WA 2, 751; LW 35, 62–63). This emphasis on the mere performance of the Eucharist, Luther explains, does not correspond to the purpose for which it was instituted:

> It was not instituted for its own sake, that it might please God, but for our sake, that we might use it right, exercise our faith by it, and through

it become pleasing to God. If it is merely an *opus operatum*, it works only harm everywhere; it must become an *opus operantis*. Just as bread and wine, no matter how much they may please God in and of themselves, work only harm if they are not used, so it is not enough that the sacrament be merely completed (that is, *opus operatum*); it must also be used in faith (that is, *opus operantis*) (*WA* 2, 751; *LW* 35, 63).

These attitudes regarding the celebration of the Eucharist seem to Luther most obvious among the so-called "Brotherhoods." Organized chiefly for devotional purposes, these were associations whose members were committed to the recitation of certain prayers and attendance at certain Masses on behalf of fellow members. This was especially true at the time when one approached death. In this way, each member participated in the benefits arising from the "good works" of all the other members.[16] These "Brotherhoods" were becoming more numerous, with members belonging to several at one time. Wittenberg itself had twenty of these fraternities. To Luther, they were catering to a craving for the assurance of salvation based only on the performance of good deeds. He complained further that, often, the members, having gathered to attend one or more Masses, spent the rest of the day in revelry (*WA* 2, 754; *LW* 35, 68). This was not the kind of Christian fellowship that he had earlier explained as the primary benefit of this sacrament!

In this treatise on the Blessed Sacrament, Luther refrains from labelling as "errors" the emphases and attitudes he criticizes. Yet we can easily detect a growing opposition to the Mass as a good work performed without attention to interior dispositions, especially the exercise of faith.

During the years 1518–1520, Luther had become increasingly critical of good works in general. At the Heidelberg Disputation in April 1518, where he proposed and defended certain important theological and philosophical theses, some of his propositions expressed a distrust of human nature and human activity while others exalted faith.[17] As Luther strengthened these correlative emphases in his sermons and lectures, it seemed that he was advocating a total neglect of

---

[16] For a brief history of these "Brotherhoods" and their practices, cf. F. Grass and G. Schreiber, "Brüderschaft," *Lexikon für Theologie und Kirche* II, cols. 719–21.
[17] McNally, "The Ninety-Five Theses of Martin Luther, 1517–1967," 467.

good works. Soon, even those sympathetic to his views urged him to clarify his position. Georg Spalatin (1484–1545), private secretary to the Elector of Saxony, Frederick the Wise (1463–1525), encouraged him to write on this subject (*WA* 6, 196). Luther complied, and the work originally intended to be in the form of a sermon to his congregation at the City Church soon became a substantial treatise, *Von den guten Werken* (1520).

At the outset, Luther wishes to make clear what he means by "good works." A good work is simply anything that has been commanded by God:

> The first thing to know is that there are no good works except those works which God has commanded, just as there is no sin except that which God has forbidden. Therefore, whoever wants to know what good works are as well as doing them needs to know nothing more than God's commandments (*WA* 6, 206; *LW* 44, 23).

Taking the wind out of the sails of his critics, Luther explains that the first and most precious of all good works is faith in Christ. When the Jews asked Christ, "What must we do to be doing the works of God?" he answered them, "This is the work of God, that you believe in him whom he has sent" (Jn. 6:28–29). Faith is a commandment of Christ and, therefore, it is a good work (*ibid.*).

Faith, in fact, is the most important good work because it also provides the climate and condition of all other works. In it, all works become equal, and one work is like another; all distinctions between works fall away, whether they be great, small, many or few. For the works are acceptable not for their own sake but because of faith, which is always the same and lives and works in each and every work without distinction (*WA* 6, 206–207; *LW* 44, 26).[18] In this perspective, the term "good works" applies to all works done in faith and not simply such specific works as praying in church, fasting and almsgiving, as his opponents maintain (*WA* 6, 205; *LW* 44, 24).

With this introduction, Luther undertakes an examination of all of the Ten Commandments, specifying the good works connected with each of them. In this investigation, his treatment of the Third

---

[18]   Robin A. Leaver, *Luther on Justification* (St. Louis, 1975), argues convincingly in this brief treatment of a vast subject for a wider meaning of "faith" in Luther.

Commandment is of special interest, for it is here that he situates the Mass as a good work according to the terms of his definition. The words of institution bid us celebrate the Eucharist as a memorial of Christ that is to our benefit:

> In these words has Christ made a memorial or an anniversary to be ob-
> served daily throughout Christendom. To it he has added a wonderful,
> rich, great testament in which are bequeathed and distributed not in-
> terest, money or temporal possessions, but the forgiveness of all sins,
> grace and mercy unto eternal life, that all who come to this memorial
> shall have the same testament. He died with the intent that this testa-
> ment become permanent and irrevocable. In proof and evidence of this
> he left his own body and blood under bread and wine, instead of letter
> and seal (WA 6, 230; LW 44, 55–56).

As he had explained it in his commentary on Hebrews, Luther again conceives the Eucharist as a testament, a will with a spiritual inher-itance in which all participate. It is also described as a memorial, a memorial of Christ's death, for he has left his own body and blood under the form of bread and wine as evidence of the testament that he has made. And since Christ bade us celebrate it, this testament, this memorial, is a good work.

An important part of the celebration of this memorial for Luther is the sermon, which ought to be nothing else but the proclamation of the testament of forgiveness contained in the memorial. Preaching the gospel in this sense is also a good work because it has been strictly commanded by Christ (WA 6, 231–32; LW 44, 57). Likewise, prayer, whether common, as part of the memorial, or private and personal, is a good work of the Third Commandment. But accepting the testament, listening to the gospel being preached, and praying, all require faith. It is again the condition of all good works. Without faith, these cease to be good works. And what Luther sees around him as a collapse of faith leads him at this point to show some polemical colours, as he compares the leaders of the Roman Church to the Turks, the enemy feared by the Church and the Empire alike:

> If the Turk destroys cities, country and people, and lays waste churches,
> we think a great injury has been done Christendom. Then we start com-
> plaining, and urge kings and princes to wage war. But when faith col-
> lapses, love grows cold, God's word is neglected, and all manner of sin

takes control, nobody thinks of fighting. In fact, pope, bishop, priests and clergy, who ought to be the generals, captains, and standard-bearers in this spiritual warfare against the Turks of a far deadlier spiritual kind, are themselves the very princes and leaders of such Turks, of a devilish army, just as Judas led the Jews when they took Christ prisoner (*WA* 6, 241–42; *LW* 44, 70).

In this treatise, Luther does clarify his meaning of the term "good works," and he indicates the sense in which he applies the term to the Mass. Like his previous writings examined so far, it does not contain a positive exposition of his doctrine which would constitute open disagreement with the Church of Rome. But Luther was moving in this direction, impelled no doubt by certain events in the wake of the Indulgence Controversy. In July of the previous year, 1519, he had met with John Eck (1486–1543) in the Leipzig Debate and was lured beyond his criticism of papal power to calling into question the authority of a general council of the Church.[19] On June 15, 1520, Leo X (pope, 1513–1521), with editorial assistance from Eck, issued a papal bull, *Exsurge Domine*, which condemned forty-one articles "found in the writings and pamphlets of a certain Martin Luther." Some of these articles are noteworthy at the present stage of this investigation:

1. It is an heretical opinion, but a common one, that the sacraments of the new law give pardoning grace to those who do not set up an obstacle.
31. In every good work the righteous man sins.
32. A good work done very well is a venial sin.
36. Free will after sin is a matter of name only; and as long as one does what is in him, one sins mortally.[20]

These and other articles, formulated without much regard for the context in which they were found in Luther's writings, would nevertheless evoke for contemporary theologians the spectres of heresies condemned by previous popes and councils of the Church.

[19] Rupp, *Luther's Progress*, pp. 67–69; cf. also Carter Lindberg, "Luther's Views on Papal Authority," *Andover Newton Quarterly* XVII (Number 3, 1977), 213–26.
[20] Hans J. Hillerbrand, *The Reformation: A Narrative History Related by Contemporary Observers and Participants* (New York, 1964), pp. 81–83. (In quotations throughout this work, exclusive language of the author/translator has been retained; in the main text, I have attempted to use inclusive language.)

An appendix to the document directed that all of Luther's writings containing these errors were to be burned, and ordered Luther to cease publishing books and pamphlets and within sixty days to prepare a formal recantation of his errors under threat of excommunication.[21] Far from heeding this edict, Luther in fact became quite prolific at this time, publishing three major treatises, all of them in more open conflict with the Roman Church, and two of them especially relevant to the present subject: *Ein Sermon von dem neuen Testament, das ist von der heiligen Messe* (July 1520), and *De captivitate Babylonica ecclesiae praeludium* (September–October 1520).[22] To the call for recantation, Luther responded dramatically on December 10 when, before a gathering of students and sympathetic professors at the Elster Gate of Wittenberg, he burned the papal bull itself, the books of Canon Law and some works of scholastic theology.[23]

Luther's treatise on the New Testament represents his first systematic effort to replace the traditional notion of the Mass as a sacrifice and good work with the evangelical teaching of the Lord's Supper as a testament. Wishing to start with the pure doctrine of Christ, he adopts the following principle: "The nearer our masses are to the first mass of Christ, the better they undoubtedly are; and the further from Christ's mass, the more dangerous" (*WA* 6, 355; *LW* 35, 81). Accordingly, if we wish to understand the Mass properly, we must disregard all the externals which have become associated with it, such as vestments, bells, songs, ornaments and so forth, and try to grasp thoroughly the words of Christ by which he instituted the Mass in the first place and commanded us to perform it (*WA* 6, 355; *LW* 35, 82). To study the words of institution for this purpose provides a firm base because the word of God is itself foundational:

> This word of God is the beginning, the foundation, the rock, upon which afterwards all works, words and thoughts of man must build. This word man must gratefully accept. He must faithfully believe the divine promise and by no means doubt that it is and comes to pass just as God promises. This trust and faith is the beginning, middle, and end of all works and righteousness (*WA* 6, 356; *LW* 35, 82).

---

[21] *Ibid.*, pp. 83–84.
[22] Earlier, in June 1520, Luther had published *An den christlichen Adel deutscher Nation von des christlichen Standes Besserung.*
[23] Rupp, *Luther's Progress*, p. 90.

In attending to the words of institution, Luther finds they contain a promise or solemn vow concerning our righteousness and our salvation. Moreover, it is a special kind of promise in the form of a testament or last will:

> Not every vow is called a testament, but only a last irrevocable will of one who is about to die, whereby he bequeaths his goods, allotted and assigned to be distributed to whom he will. Just as St. Paul says to the Hebrews (9:16–17) that a testament must be made operative by death, and is not in effect while the one still lives who made the testament (WA 6, 357; LW 35, 84).

This testament is called the "New" Testament in Christ's own blood, because it replaces and makes obsolete the Old Testament established by Moses. Here, Luther conceives even the Old Testament as a "will" because it was a promise made through Moses to the people of Israel concerning their possession of the land of Canaan. For this testament or will, God did not die, but the paschal lamb had to die instead of Christ and as a type of Christ (*ibid.*).

Returning to the New Testament and the promise it contains, we may ask with Luther: "What then is this testament, or what is bequeathed to us in it by Christ?" Luther answers with his own straightforward exegesis of the words of institution:

> Truly a great, eternal, and unspeakable treasure, namely the forgiveness of all sins, as the words plainly state, "This is the cup of a new, eternal testament in my blood, which is poured out for you and for many for the forgiveness of sins." It is as if Christ were saying, "See here, man, in these words I promise and bequeath to you forgiveness of all your sins and life eternal. In order that you may be certain and know that such a promise remains irrevocably yours, I will die for it, and will give my body and blood for it, and will leave them both to you as a sign and seal, that by them you may remember me" (WA 6, 358; LW 35, 85).

Luther's explanation of the promise is basically the same here as that given in *Von den guten Werken*, including the permanent validation of the promise by Christ's death and its sign given in his body and blood under the form of bread and wine. In elaborating on the sign, however, Luther explains that though it be external, yet it contains and signifies something spiritual; the external which we grasp with the eyes of the body draws us to the spiritual which we comprehend with the eyes of the heart (*WA* 6, 359; *LW* 35, 86). This would seem to be a richer concept of sacrament than we noted earlier in his *Sermon von dem hoch-würdigen Sakrament*, where the term designated only the external sign.

In summary, then, the Mass as a testament contains all the elements of a last will: the testator is Christ, the heirs are Christian believers, the terms of the testament are contained in the words of Christ, the words of institution. The body and blood of Christ, as bread and wine, are the seal of the testament, the remission of sins and eternal life are the bequeathed blessings, and we remember the testament by preaching to the faithful these inherited blessings, expressive of Christ's love and grace (*WA* 6, 359–60; *LW* 35, 86–87). One listens to this preaching, and accepts and receives this testament in faith, relying on the living words of Christ and desiring what he has promised in them (*WA* 6, 361; *LW* 35, 88–89).

But for Luther the Mass as celebrated in 1520 once again bore little resemblance to this understanding of the Eucharist. In the first place, the words of the testament containing the promise and inheritance are wrapped in silence. They are secret words spoken privately in the Mass by the priest only. But the words of institution are the central part of the Mass just as the words are important for any of the sacraments. Without them, the sacraments are dead and empty, like a body without a soul, a cask without wine, a purse without money (*WA* 6, 363; *LW* 35, 91). Furthermore, without words, there can be no response in faith, and then works substitute for faith:

> It must necessarily follow where faith and the word or promise of God decline or are neglected, that in their place there arise works and a false, presumptuous trust in them. For where there is no promise of God, there is no faith. Where there is no faith, there everyone presumptuously undertakes to better himself and make himself well pleasing to God by means of works (*WA* 6, 364; *LW* 35, 92).

When the words of the testament are spoken secretly, there is danger that the Mass itself becomes a work by which one tries to make oneself pleasing to God. But this is to pervert the foregoing explanation of the true Mass:

> Now if we have properly understood what has been said above, namely, that the mass is nothing else than a testament and sacrament in which God makes a pledge to us and gives us grace and mercy, I think it is

not fitting that we should make a good work or merit out of it. For a
testament is not *beneficium acceptum, sed datum*; it does not take benefit
from us, but brings benefit to us. Who has ever heard that he who
receives an inheritance has done a good work? He simply takes for himself
a benefit. Likewise in the mass we give nothing to Christ, but only
receive from him; unless they are willing to call this a good work, that
a person sits still and permits himself to be benefited, given food and
drink, clothed and healed, helped and redeemed (*WA* 6, 364; *LW* 35,
93).

Merely to accept the testament as a benefit is not a good work, and
yet this is the most important function in assisting at the Eucharist.
True, when we come together for the celebration we say prayers and
distribute alms to the poor, and these, if they are done in faith, are
good works. But work and prayer are distinct from the testament and
sacrament, and must be kept separate from them (*WA* 6, 364–65;
LW 35, 93–94).

A second major misunderstanding of the Eucharist, Luther maintains, is to regard the Mass as a sacrifice, as something that is offered
to God. This impression is given by some of the prayers and ceremonies
of the Mass, especially at the ritualistic offertory. But here again we
must separate clearly and distinctly the prayers and ceremonies, which
have been added to the Mass by the holy Fathers, from the testament
and sacrament comprehended in the words of Christ (*WA* 6, 367;
LW 35, 97). Is there any offering, then, in the Mass? Yes, says Luther,
we offer ourselves; we yield ourselves to the will of God that he may
make of us what he wishes, according to his own pleasure. In addition,
we offer him praise and thanksgiving with our whole heart for his grace
and mercy, which he has promised and given us in this sacrament
(*WA* 6, 368; *LW* 35, 98). But we do not make this offering on our
own behalf; we offer ourselves as a sacrifice along with Christ. In the
Mass, therefore, we do not offer Christ as a sacrifice but Christ offers
us. Luther explains:

> That is, we lay ourselves on Christ by a firm faith in his testament and
> do not otherwise appear before God with our prayer, praise and sacrifice
> except through Christ and his mediation. Nor do we doubt that Christ
> is our priest or minister in heaven before God. Such faith, truly, brings
> it to pass that Christ takes up our cause, presents us and our prayer and
> praise, and also offers himself for us in heaven. If the mass were so under-

stood and for this reason called a sacrifice, it would be well (*WA* 6, 369; *LW* 35, 99).

This restricted meaning of the Mass as a sacrifice has important implications for Luther. Christ, in offering us, our prayers and thanksgiving, becomes our priest and our mediator in heaven. But since we join in this oblation by offering ourselves in faith, we, too, are in some sense priests. It is not, then, the priest alone who offers the sacrifice of the Mass; it is rather each one who participates in faith. This is the true priestly office through which Christ is offered as a sacrifice to God, an office which the priest, with the outward ceremonies of the Mass, simply represents. Each and all are equally spiritual priests before God (*WA* 6, 370; *LW* 35, 100–101). In this sense, those who believe may even be said "to offer Christ," "that is, we move Christ and give him occasion to offer himself for us and to offer us with himself" (*WA* 6, 371; *LW* 35, 102). The wording here is admittedly vague and it is not clear whether this "offering," like the works of prayer and almsgiving, ought also to be considered, according to Luther, as separate from the testament and sacrament.

Secondly, since the offering is made in faith, and faith is peculiar to each individual, the benefits derived from the offering cannot be applied to another. As Luther sees it, just as one cannot give or receive the sacrament of baptism, of penance, of extreme unction, in the place of another or for his benefit, so also no one can observe or hear Mass for another, but each one for himself alone (*WA* 6, 365; *LW* 35, 94). This would seem to rule out Masses offered for the souls in purgatory. But as yet, Luther does not take a hard line in this matter; he simply registers his own doubts in view of his present understanding of the Eucharist:

> I cannot conceive that the institution of so many masses and requiems can be without abuse, especially since all this is done as good works and sacrifices by which to recompense God, whereas in the mass there is nothing else than the reception and enjoyment of divine grace, promised and given us in his testament and sacrament (*WA* 6, 371; *LW* 35, 102).

As an alternative to offering many Masses for the departed, Luther suggests instead that the faithful come together for the Eucharist and, with priestly faith which should accompany every urgent request, pray for the souls of the departed, in Christ and with Christ, not doubting that they will be heard (*WA* 6, 372; *LW* 35, 103).

Towards the end of the treatise, Luther anticipates the logical objection: since the Mass, in every important aspect, depends upon the faith of each individual believer, and since faith is internal, why should one bother with its external celebration at all? In reply, Luther lists a number of reasons why this external element of the sacrament is important. First, it is an aid to belief: we would soon cease thinking of this sacrament and testament if it were not visibly administered in certain designated places and churches. Secondly, God has, after all, instituted this sacrament; we must, therefore, receive it with great reverence, praise and gratitude (*WA* 6, 372–73; *LW* 35, 104–105). Finally, and most importantly, by celebrating the Mass with outward ceremony, the word of God is proclaimed, the gospel of God's grace and of the forgiveness of sin is preached because this central message is contained in the words of institution (*WA* 6, 373–74; *LW* 35, 105–106).

We see, then, that this treatise on the Mass presents a comprehensive and positive understanding of what Luther will begin to call the sacrament of the Lord's Supper. Though he will still call it the "Mass," it will be a Mass based upon the word of God and not upon human traditions. As yet, the distinguishing marks between this Mass and the Roman Mass remain somewhat blurred. In his next treatise published within a matter of months, *De captivitate Babylonica*, the distinctions come into sharper focus. This work is commonly regarded as an irrevocable step taken by Luther in his opposition to Rome: written in Latin rather than in German and, therefore, addressed primarily to the clergy rather than to the laity, it aimed its criticism at the whole sacramental system of the Roman Church (*WA* 6, 484).

The title alludes to the theme: just as the Jews were taken into captivity in a foreign land under the tyranny of the Babylonian Empire, so Christians have been removed from the Scriptures and have become enslaved under the tyranny of the papacy, the modern Babylon. This tyranny has been exercised by the misuse of the sacraments, particularly the Lord's Supper. In this case, a three-fold captivity has prevailed: the withholding of the cup from the laity; the teaching of transubstantiation; and the doctrine of the sacrifice of the Mass (*LW* 36, 6–7). Luther's treatment of this last captivity will now be examined.

Luther leaves little doubt, in denying at the outset that there are seven sacraments, that his target is the sacramental system. At the present time he can allow only three because only three are justified by Scripture: baptism, penance, and the bread. And if one were to examine the usage of Scripture closely, it would be more accurate to say that there is only one single sacrament (presumably, Christ) with three sacramental signs (*WA* 6, 501; *LW* 36, 18). Further, with regard to the sacrament of the bread, Luther eliminates from the beginning any discussion of the sixth chapter of John's gospel: it does not refer to this sacrament in a single syllable, but speaks rather of faith in the incarnate Word (*WA* 6, 502; *LW* 36, 19).

The principal abuse of the Mass consists in the opinion that it is a good work and a sacrifice. To this a host of other abuses are connected. Faith in the sacrament is thereby destroyed and it is converted into a profit-making business (*WA* 6, 512; *LW* 36, 35). Against this generally-held misconception, Luther sets out again his understanding of the true Mass. Following closely on the *Sermon von dem neuen Testament*, his exposition here contains many of the same elements. New or expanded emphases will be especially highlighted here.

The starting point for a proper understanding of the Eucharist is again the words of institution. These reveal that the Mass is a testament which, although being already an interpretation of the words, now becomes for Luther the foundation of all other considerations of the Eucharist:

> Let this stand, therefore, as our first and infallible proposition—the mass or Sacrament of the Altar is Christ's testament, which he left behind him at his death to be distributed among his believers. For that is the meaning of his words, "This cup is the new testament in my blood" (Luke 22:20; I Cor. 11:25). Let this truth stand, I say, as the immovable foundation on which we shall base all that we have to say (*WA* 6, 513; *LW* 36, 37).

The testament is, therefore, a last will, a promise made by one about to die, in which he designates his bequest and appoints his heirs. This promise of Christ in the sacrament is related to all of the promises of God made from the beginning of the world; from it, all these previous promises derive their value. Hence, the implication of these promises was that God would one day die. But God could not die unless he became human. Thus, the incarnation and death of Christ are both comprehended by the word "testament" (*WA* 6, 513–14; *LW* 36, 38). For Luther, then, the incarnation makes possible the fulfillment of all

the promises in the Old Testament and is directly linked to the manner
in which the atonement for humanity would be achieved.

Since the Mass is essentially a promise, we share it, have access to it,
not by works or powers or merits of our own, but by faith alone:

> Where there is the Word of the promising God, there must necessarily
> be the faith of the accepting man. It is plain, therefore, that the begin-
> ning of our salvation is a faith which clings to the Word of the promising
> God, who, without any effort on our part, in free and unmerited mercy
> takes the initiative and offers us the word of this promise (WA 6, 514;
> LW 36, 39).

Here, our response to the sacrament is placed in the broader context
of the movement towards justification, but the response is the same:
faith. And the total response is not *only* faith, for after faith comes love;
then love does every good work and is the fulfilling of the law. Luther's
expression at this point borders on the mystical:

> Hard on this faith there follows, of itself, a most sweet stirring of the
> heart, whereby the spirit of man is enlarged and enriched (that is love,
> given by the Holy Spirit through faith in Christ), so that he is drawn to
> Christ, that gracious and bounteous testator, and made a thoroughly
> new and different man (WA 6, 515; LW 36, 40).

These words indicate that faith, however important initially in our
response to God's word in the promise, is not the only ingredient in
that response. Further, the final words, "a thoroughly new and different
man," suggest that Luther, at least at this stage of his theological development, did not look upon justification as something external, as
merely the imputation of the righteousness of God.[24] The process of
justification is related to the testament because the promise contained
therein, of the forgiveness of sin and eternal life, is the sum and substance of the gospel message (WA 6, 525; LW 36, 56).

To assist us in responding in faith to the promise, an external sign
is provided. Like other previous promises of God, the sacrament of
the Eucharist has its sign:

---

[24] Leaver, *Luther on Justification*, pp. 62–63, finds Luther holding to inherent justification even in his later (1535) *Lectures on Galatians*. Cf. on the same point, using other
references as well, Jared Wicks, "Justification and Faith in Luther," *Theological Studies*
XLIV (March 1983), 23–24.

> . . . in every promise of God two things are presented to us, the word
> and the sign, so that we are to understand the word to be the testament,
> but the sign to be the sacrament. Thus in the mass, the word of Christ
> is the testament, and the bread and wine are the sacrament. And as there
> is greater power in the word than in the sign, so there is greater power
> in the testament than in the sacrament; for a man can have or use the
> word or testament apart from the sign or sacrament. "Believe," says St.
> Augustine, "and you have eaten" (WA 6, 518; LW 36, 44).

The sign is integral to the promise, but is of less importance than the
word or testament. In the Mass, the sign is the bread and wine, and
again Luther refers to the elements as *sacramentum*, although only in
conjunction with word and testament.

Turning to the consideration of current Mass practice, Luther lists
many of the deficiencies that he had noted in *Von dem neuen Testament*.
The words of institution are not announced to the laity but pronounced
in secret by the priests at the consecration (WA 6, 516; LW 36, 41).
Faith is thereby extinguished and in its place follows the godless superstition of works: prayers, preparations, works, signs, gestures—
these fill the vacuum. But without faith, they become exercises of
impiety rather than of piety (WA 6, 517; LW 36, 42).

On the objection to the Mass as a good work, Luther is more explicit
than in previous writings:

> You have seen that the mass is nothing else than the divine promise or
> testament of Christ, sealed with the sacrament of his body and blood.
> If that is true, you will understand that it cannot possibly be in any way
> a work; nobody can possibly do anything in it, neither can it be dealt
> with in any other way than by faith alone. However, faith is not a work,
> but the lord and life of all works (WA 6, 520; LW 36, 47).

The Mass as testament is directed to us; it is something given to us.
By accepting it in faith we do not do anything with it. Our acceptance
of it cannot be a good work; nor can it be a good work for anyone else.
Faith is personal and, therefore, the benefits of the Mass can only be
communicated to us who believe with personal faith (WA 6, 521;
LW 36, 48). True, prayers may be said for one another when the people
gather together for the Mass; and prayers said in faith, the "lord and
life of all works," are good works. But, Luther insists again, such prayers are separate from the Mass as testament (WA 6, 522; LW 36, 50).

When this distinction is not kept in mind, the Mass itself comes to be regarded as a good work.

A second stumbling block (and it is significant that Luther considers it a "second" stumbling block) to the true doctrine of the Mass is the common belief that the Mass is a sacrifice. According to this belief, Christ is offered to God the Father as an all-sufficient sacrifice in the celebration of the Mass. In refutation, Luther invokes the principle that he had formulated earlier: the closer the Mass resembles the first Mass instituted by Christ, the more Christian it will be. But when Christ instituted the Mass at the Last Supper, he did not offer himself to God the Father; he set forth the testament for those present and offered to them a sign of this testament. It was a simple ceremony, without any display of vestments or gestures. So, if the Mass was intended to be a sacrifice, then we must say that Christ's institution of it was not complete (*WA* 6, 523; *LW* 36, 52). But from the manner of its institution, it simply cannot be a sacrifice for the more basic reason that the Mass as testament and the Mass as sacrifice are contradictory affirmations:

> Therefore, just as distributing a testament or accepting a promise differs diametrically from offering a sacrifice, so it is a contradiction in terms to call the mass a sacrifice, for the former is something that we receive and the latter is something that we give. The same thing cannot be received and offered at the same time, nor can it be both given and accepted by the same person, any more than our prayer can be the same thing as that which our prayer obtains, or the act of praying be the same thing as the act of receiving that for which we pray (*WA* 6, 523–24; *LW* 36, 52).

It may be noted here that Luther seems to restrict the institution of the Mass to the Last Supper, apart from Christ's death and sacrifice of himself. As in the last treatise examined, he allows for some "offerings" at the Mass as almsgiving, collections of food and drink to be distributed to those in need; but these have no reference to the sacrament and testament (*WA* 6, 524; *LW* 36, 53). He here omits mention of any offering of ourselves in the Mass, thus limiting further the sense in which "sacrifice" can be associated with the Eucharist.

In a summary statement, Luther makes clear the opposition he sees between the Mass as a testament and the Mass as sacrifice and good work:

Therefore these two things—mass and prayer, sacrament and work, testament and sacrifice—must not be confused; for the one comes from
God to us through the ministration of the priest and demands our faith,
the other proceeds from our faith to God through the priest and demands
his hearing. The former descends, the latter ascends (*WA* 6, 526; *LW*
36, 56).

Mass, sacrament, testament imply a movement-to-us; prayer, work,
sacrifice imply a movement-to-God. Luther does not further distin-
guish "work" and "sacrifice"; but this analysis so far would indicate
that, in relation to the Mass as sacrament or testament, he understands
"work" (or "good work") as something done in faith to obtain a benefit
from God, either for oneself or another, and "sacrifice" as something
offered to God as gift.

In the remainder of the treatise, Luther exposes the tyranny of the
Church with respect to the other sacraments. Only a few points need
to be observed here as having relevance to the subject of this study. In
treating the sacrament of penance, Luther has an admirable defence of
the practice of private confession (*WA* 6, 546; *LW* 36, 86).[25] Yet penance as a sacrament is not supported by the Scriptures; consequently,
at the end of the treatise Luther sanctions only two sacraments, baptism
and the bread—a modification of his position at the beginning. In
treating the sacrament of ordination, Luther assures Christians that
they are all equally priests, that is, they have the same power with
respect to the word and the sacraments. The "sacrament" of ordination
is nothing else but a certain rite whereby one is called to the ministry
of the Church (*WA* 6, 566; *LW* 36, 116).

By the end of 1520, the main outlines of Luther's evangelical understanding of the Eucharist were sketched. In his earlier exegetical
writings, some aspects of the sacrament were questioned. In conjunction with formulating the defence of his position on other doctrines
and under the pressure of events escalating his conflict with Rome,
Luther perused the Scriptures for the foundations of the Eucharist and
the other sacraments. Taking as his motto Paul's dictum, "Test everything; hold fast to what is good" (I Thess. 5:21), Luther soon had

---

[25] Thomas N. Tentler treats Luther's reform of the medieval doctrine and discipline of
      the sacrament of penance in *Sin and Confession on the Eve of the Reformation* (Princeton,
      1977), pp. 349–62.

enough evidence to devote a separate treatise to the Mass or, as he referred to it in the title, the "New Testament." This treatise, together with his elaborations on the same subject in *De captivitate Babylonica*, signalled Luther's challenge to the traditional understanding of the Mass as sacrifice.

CHAPTER II
1521–1525

he bonfire incident at Wittenberg on December 10, 1520, was Luther's answer to Pope Leo's demand for him to recant his errors within sixty days. Kept informed on the worsening situation in Germany by his envoy Jerome Aleander (1480–1542), Leo countered with a definitive response in the bull, *Decet Romanum Pontificem*, on January 3, 1521, in which Luther was officially excommunicated from the Catholic Church.[1]

On October 23, 1520, Charles V (1500–1558) had been crowned king at Aachen, succeeding Maximilian I who had died on January 12, 1519. In the course of the coronation ceremony, Charles was required to assure the basic rights of the Church and Empire by responding to a number of questions. One question read, "Will you keep and advance our traditional, holy, Catholic faith?"[2] On the basis of his affirmative answer, Charles was faced with the problem that Luther's excommunication posed: should this canonical sentence be affirmed by the Empire? The young emperor did not want to condemn a German subject without prior investigation. Thus, after initial hesitation and uncertainty he invited Luther to appear at the forthcoming Diet of Worms for a hearing of his case, and issued him a writ of safe conduct.[3] Luther accepted and made his way to Worms, arriving in the city on April 16, 1521. On the following days, he appeared before the imperial

[1] Rupp, *Luther's Progress*, p. 93; Hendrix, *Luther and the Papacy*, p. 123.
[2] Lortz, *The Reformation*, I, pp. 309–10.
[3] *Ibid.*, p. 312.

Diet. He was asked to acknowledge whether in fact he was the author of the works on display, and he was ordered to recant the errors contained in them. While willing to admit that he had been too polemical at times, Luther stood by the positions that he had already taken regarding the power and doctrine of the papacy. Appealing to the word of God and his own conscience, he uttered his dramatic and final refusal to recant.[4]

In the name of the Diet, Charles V issued the Edict of Worms in May 1521. After listing Luther's errors and reviewing the efforts made to bring him to recant the same, it declared that he be considered "an estranged member, rotten and cut off from the body of our Holy Mother Church . . . an obstinate, schismatic heretic. . . ."[5] No one was to offer him hospitality; rather, he was to be taken prisoner. Luther left Worms before the Edict was published and, after visiting relatives at Möhra, he was apprehended, possibly by friendly forces, and taken to the Castle Wartburg near Eisenach where he would remain until March 1522.[6]

Luther's stay at the Wartburg was a period of retirement from the public eye for him. But retirement did not mean inactivity! He set to work on a German translation of the New Testament and continued his output of treatises on theological topics. He wrote once again on the Mass, *Vom Missbrauch der Messe*, and on monastic vows. Reflecting ten years later, Luther marvels that he was ever courageous enough to attack these two pillars of the papacy:

> Others before me, like Erasmus, criticized the life that people lived under the papacy, but I never thought I would be able to attack the two pillars on which the papacy rests, the mass and the (monastic) vows, for to do so seemed to me like an attack on God and his creation (*WA TR* 1, 42; *LW* 54, 13).[7]

---

[4] *Ibid.*, pp. 317–18.

[5] Jensen, *Confrontation at Worms,* p. 101. An original French edition of the Edict, with an English translation, is here supplied, pp. 73–111.

[6] Lortz, *The Reformation*, I, p. 320. Although the Edict was issued in the name of the assembled Electors and Princes, the effectiveness of its decrees was weakened for two reasons, according to Lortz, *ibid.*, p. 321: first, the Diet had already disbanded and many participants had returned home before the decrees were ratified; secondly, the Edict was not included in the official resolutions of the *Reichstag*.

[7] *WA TR*, abbreviation for *D. Martin Luthers Werke, Krit. Gesamtausgabe. Tischreden* (Weimar, 1912ff.).

Perhaps the events that have just been recalled at the beginning of this
chapter, culminating in Luther's excommunication, gave him a feeling
of freedom and enabled him to lay aside any lingering inhibitions in
his criticism of the papacy. It is difficult to relate this quotation from
his *Table Talk* to any definite period of his career. And yet one notices
in his treatises after 1521 how he advances his arguments with less
caution and more invective.

Vom Missbrauch der Messe was written towards the end of 1521 in both
Latin and German.[8] Addressed to the Augustinian friars at Wittenberg, it may have been intended as an aid to some crucial discussions
that they were holding at this time on the Mass, centring on topics
such as the Mass as a good work, the so-called private Mass, and Communion under both kinds (*WA* 8, 404–405). But like his other works,
it was soon in the publisher's hands and in early 1522 it became available to both his followers and his critics.

Luther begins this treatise by explaining the kind of priesthood necessary for administering the sacrament of the Eucharist. He appeals
principally to Scripture in his arguments. In the New Testament, there
is simply no outward, visible priesthood. Texts such as I Pet. 3:18—
"For Christ also died for sins once for all, the righteous for the un-
righteous, that he might bring us to God . . . "—state clearly that
there is only one priest, Christ, who has sacrificed himself for us. His
was the only visible priesthood. There is, of course, a spiritual priesthood in which all Christians share and through which they are all priests
with Christ: "You are a chosen race, a royal priesthood, a holy nation,
God's own people" (I Pet. 2:9). But for this priesthood, according to
Luther, there is no need of anointed or ordained priests; no priest or
mediator besides Christ is necessary (*WA* 8, 486; *LW* 36, 138).

But is Scripture the only basis for establishing the nature of the priesthood? According to tradition, whatever the Church establishes is
established by God because it has his Spirit. Consequently, if the
Church establishes a visible priesthood for worship, then such a priesthood is validly established. This objection completely reverses the
proper priority which, for Luther, the word of God should have:

---

[8]   Its title in Latin is *De abroganda missa privata Martini Lutheri sententia*. Since it was the
German version that was reprinted and more widely circulated, the controversy on the
Mass continued on the basis of its arguments. Consequently this version will be ana-
lysed in the text.

> It is not God's Word just because the church speaks it; rather, the church
> comes into being because God's Word is spoken. The church does not
> constitute the Word, but is constituted by the Word. A sure sign, by
> which we know where the church is, is the Word of God, as St. Paul
> writes . . . (I Cor. 14:24–25) (WA 8, 491; LW 36, 144–45).

The word constitutes the Church; the Church does not constitute the
word. This principle, fundamental to Luther's developing notion of
ecclesiology, is more than adequate for his present purpose: what the
word says about the nature of the priesthood is to be believed rather
than what the Church teaches about it.

Since for Luther there is no visible priesthood, there can be no sacrifice. Therefore, sacrifices and works that are effected by the papal
priesthood are of no value. The pope's law, which establishes such a
priesthood, abrogates the law of Christ; it is a deceit and a falsehood.
Then the Mass, the sacrifice of this priesthood, worse than being of no
value, becomes idolatry and a grave misuse of the sacrament (WA 8,
489; LW 36, 142). With this misuse of the body and blood of Christ
occurring daily, the wonder is that God has been patient for so long,
and has withheld his wrath and punishment. But the day of wrath will
come (WA 8, 490; LW 36, 143).

There remain, however, legitimate sacrifices: the spiritual sacrifice of
our bodies, recommended by Paul (Rom. 12:1), and the sacrifice of
praise and thanksgiving (Heb. 13:15–16). But these are offered by *all*
Christians; hence, all who offer them are priests (WA 8, 492; LW 36,
145). It is not clear from the context whether Luther, as formerly,
associates these sacrifices with a liturgical service. What is clear is that
any Christian may offer them; they do not depend upon the special
competence of clerics. Later in his treatise, in fact, Luther states that
even the specific acts of the ministry, that is, preaching the word and
administering the sacraments, are entrusted to a person as an office that
alone distinguishes him from a layperson:

> There is no essential difference between bishops, elders, and priests on
> the one hand and laymen on the other, nothing to distinguish them from
> other Christians except that the one has a different office which is en-
> trusted to him, namely, to preach the Word of God and to administer
> the sacraments; just as a mayor or judge is distinguished from other
> citizens by nothing except that the governing of the city is entrusted to
> him (WA 8, 503; LW 36, 159).

Much less, of course, is there any distinction between the orders of priest, elder and bishop. The office of bishop, with jurisdiction over several cities, is without basis in Scripture. Bishops are by the appointment of the devil and his apostle, the pope (*WA* 8, 501; *LW* 36, 156–57).

In his more positive treatment of the sacrament of the Eucharist itself, Luther again anchors his position firmly in Scripture with a more extensive exegesis of the accounts of its institution than he has given so far. He deals with the separable parts of the scriptural accounts in reverse order. Christ's injunction to the apostles, "Do this in remembrance of me" (I Cor. 11:24–25), means simply to do what he had just done: he took bread and wine and with the words that he spoke made of them his body and blood and gave them to the apostles to eat and drink. He did not use a gold chalice or gold vestments nor did he surround his actions with elaborate ceremonies (*WA* 8, 509; *LW* 36, 166). The words of institution that Christ spoke—"This is my body . . . . This cup . . . is the new covenant in my blood" (Lk. 22:19–20)—express the promise of his body and the pouring out of his blood for the remission of sins. To the promise belongs faith, that is, the conviction that we shall receive what is promised to us (*WA* 8, 511; *LW* 36, 169). There is no trace here of sacrifice. A sacrifice is a work in which we present and give to God something of our own. But the promise here is God's word, which gives us the grace and mercy of God (*WA* 8, 512; *LW* 36, 169). Similarly, the introductory words of the institution narrative, "He took bread, and when he had given thanks he broke it and gave it to them" (Lk. 22:19), do not carry any sacrificial intention. "Gave it to them" is surely not the same as "offering it to God"; "to take" (for oneself) is different from "to offer" to another (*WA* 8, 513; *LW* 36, 170).

So far the context of Luther's exposition of the sacrament is the Last Supper. Does the Eucharist have any reference to the death of Christ? This dimension does receive some attention from Luther. In partaking of the sacrament, we observe a memorial of Christ and proclaim his death. By eating the bread and drinking the wine, we keep the sacrament for ourselves; we consume it. It is obvious then, for Luther, that we do not sacrifice it; what is less obvious (from what Luther says) is that, by doing the same thing, we "proclaim his death." A clearer reference of the sacrament to Christ's death is to be found in the sign, the pledge and seal of the promise:

> In order that we may be certain of this promise of Christ and truly rely
> on it without any doubt, he has given us the most precious and costly
> seal and pledge, his true body and blood under bread and wine—the
> very same as that with which he obtained for us the gift and promise of
> this precious and gracious treasure, surrendering his life that we might
> receive and accept the promised grace (WA 8, 516; LW 36, 174).

The promise, with this sign, becomes a testament because it was given
by Christ as he was about to die.

If the sacrament as a testament implies the death of Christ, this does
not make it a sacrifice. It keeps its essential character as something
that God bequeaths to us, not something we sacrifice to him. And to
call it a sacrifice is to call God a liar, since he himself referred to it as
a testament (WA 8, 521; LW 36, 180). Moreover, were the sacrament
a sacrifice rather than a testament, we would have to revise our concept
of God. He who sacrifices wishes to reconcile God; to reconcile God
supposes that he is angry and unmerciful. But to receive from him his
greatest treasure, the remission of sins and eternal life, as a testament,
presupposes that we approach God as one who is both kind and gracious
(WA 8, 517; LW 36, 175). God has already been reconciled. The body
of Christ was given and his blood poured out for us, to avert the wrath
of God which we deserved by our sins. By this act of Christ, the wrath
is gone, and our sins are forgiven; were it not for this act, God would
still be angry, and we would remain in our sins (WA 8, 519; LW 36,
177).

Luther next anticipates two objections. What about the Canon, the
principal prayer of the Mass, which refers plainly to "these gifts,
holy and unspotted sacrifices," and to "a holy offering, a pure offering
and an unspotted offering"? The Canon, Luther replies, was composed
by some babbler who did not have the Spirit of God. It is, therefore,
a human word and work that must yield to the gospel and the Holy
Spirit (WA 8, 526–27; LW 36, 185–86).[9] What about the holy Fathers
of the Church, such as Gregory, Bernard, Bonaventure, who have used
the Canon and considered the Mass a sacrifice?

> To this I answer that nothing is more dangerous than the works and
> lives of the saints which are not founded in the Scriptures. Since it is

---

9   For Luther's critique of the Canon and its implications, cf. Rudolf Padberg, "Luther
    und der Canon Missae," *Catholica* XXXVII (No. 4, 1983), 288–305.

evident that the righteous man falls seven times (Prov. 24:16) and the saints sin in many ways, who will convince us that this which they have practiced and carried out without the Scriptures is not a sin? (*WA* 8, 527; *LW* 36, 186).

Although the saints err in straying from the Scriptures, they nevertheless have faith in Christ and this preserves them. They are to be imitated in this faith, not in what they do, that is, their works.

In the last part of *Vom Missbrauch*, Luther takes up again—with a more polemical touch—the subject of the priesthood. Only two priesthoods have been instituted by God: the outward priesthood in the Old Testament in which Aaron was the high priest; and the Christian, spiritual priesthood in which the high priest is Christ alone (*WA* 8, 539; *LW* 36, 200). The law of the priesthood of Christ is faith—a living, spiritual flame, by which hearts are set afire, born anew and converted through the Holy Spirit. Its sacrifice is the living sacrifice of Christ; his body was sacrificed once on the cross, while our bodies are sacrificed daily as a living, holy sacrifice (Rom. 12:1) (*WA* 8, 539; *LW* 36, 200–201). In sharp contrast to this priesthood stands the papal priesthood. Its high priest is the pope; its law is canon law; and its sacrifice is the sacrament of the altar and money (*WA* 8, 554; *LW* 36, 218).[10] The pope has changed the law and the priesthood of Christ and substituted his own law and priesthood. It is because of this usurpation that Luther referred to the pope at the beginning of the treatise in such harsh words:

> The desolating sacrilege stands in the holy place (Matt. 24:15) and rules over us in place of Christ; instead of Christ, the king of truth, stands the idol of lies and all error (II Thess. 2:3–12) (*WA* 8, 486; *LW* 36, 138).

The pope has become the desolating sacrilege, the anti-Christ.

---

[10] Luther extends the contrast further. In the following quotation, the first member refers to the priesthood of Christ, the second to the priesthood of the pope:
"Gutte werck dem nehsten dienen. / Gutte werck sich euszerlich
from stellen mit singen, fasten und betten.
Die sunde disz nach lassen. / Die sunde disz nach lassen.
Straff ewiger todt. / Straff der erdichte bann.
Lohn ewig leben. / Lohn frid und gutt diszer wellt.
Diener die prediger des wortt gotts. / Diener verkundiger der bullen.
Der brauch das Creutz mit freuden tragen. / Der brauch bösze gewissen"
(*WA* 8, 554).

In these dire circumstances, Luther exhorts his fellow friars not to offer Mass when motivated merely by a sense of duty or obligation, much less by the endowment fee. They may continue to offer Mass provided it be for the single motive of true faith (*WA* 8, 560; *LW* 36, 226). The true Mass, according to the manner and form in which it was instituted by Christ, should be revived and held each Sunday, but only once. To it, all believing Christians who hunger to be righteous should come; all who lead a carnal life should be excluded (*WA* 8, 537; *LW* 36, 198).

Throughout the treatise, Luther has relied heavily upon Scripture as the basis for his arguments. A guiding premise has been that everything which occurs outside of Scripture, especially in matters pertaining to God, comes from the devil (*WA* 8, 499; *LW* 36, 154). But to argue positively from Scripture, since it involves interpretation, has its moments of personal anguish, as Luther himself admitted in a striking passage near the beginning of *Vom Missbrauch*:

> O with how much greater effort and labor, even on the basis of Holy Scriptures, have I been barely able to justify my own conscience; so that I, one man alone, have dared to come forward against the pope, brand him as the Antichrist, the bishops as his apostles, and the universities as his brothels! How often did my heart quail, punish me, and reproach me with its single strongest argument: Are you the only wise man? (*WA* 8, 482–83; *LW* 36, 134).

More often than not, however, Luther was strengthened and confirmed in his reliance upon the word of the gospel. Later in the treatise, for example, he humbly confesses, echoing St. Paul (Eph. 3:8–10), "that to us of all people it has been given to see the pure and original face of the gospel" (*WA* 8, 562; *LW* 36, 229).

In the year following his return from the Wartburg, on March 1, 1522, Luther published three short pieces that refer briefly to the Mass as sacrifice. Two of them were written in response to other works. *Contra Henricum Regem Angliae* (July 1522) was Luther's answer to Henry VIII's *Assertio Septem Sacramentorum* (1521), which merited for Henry the title *Defensor Fidei* from Leo X.[11]

---

[11] Louis O'Donovan, ed., *Assertio Septem Sacramentorum* (New York, 1908), p. 168, cites Leo in the bull conferring the title: ". . . having found in this Book most admirable Doctrine, sprinkled with the Dew of Divine Grace . . . ." It is doubtful, however, whether Henry was its real author and the question of its authorship still remains obscure. Cf. Erwin Doernberg, *Henry VIII and Luther* (London, 1961), p. 23.

In defending the sacramental system against Luther's critique in *De captivitate Babylonica*, Henry had defended the sacrificial nature of the Eucharist. He argued that the Mass is indeed a good work: it cannot be denied that Christ, in instituting the Mass, did a good work; the priest, in offering the Mass, does what Christ did; therefore it is a good work.[12] Luther replied in terms now familiar to us, indicating that the Mass is nothing more than God's promise accompanied by an appropriate sign, and concluded:

> It is very clear that the Mass is not a matter of our work or word, but of Christ alone giving us both the word of promise and the sign of bread and wine, and that its celebration consists not in offering or sacrificing, but only in receiving and benefiting (*WA* 10[2], 212; my translation).

Furthermore, Henry failed to see how Luther could dismiss the Mass as a sacrifice, when so many Fathers of the Church and other witnesses had interpreted the words and example of Christ to mean that it precisely is a sacrifice.[13] Luther had already anticipated this argument in *Vom Missbrauch* and dismissed it as summarily here: "God cannot err or deceive; Augustine and Cyprian, as all the elect, could have erred and have erred" (*WA* 10[2], 215; my translation). The word of God, not human traditions, remains his firm foundation.

During Luther's absence from Wittenberg, liturgical reform was moving forward quickly under the impetuous leadership of Andreas Karlstadt (c. 1480–1541) and Gabriel Zwilling (c. 1487–1558). On Christmas Eve, 1521, Karlstadt had officiated at the Eucharist without vestments and distributed Communion under both species.[14] In his sermons he deprecated the use of images and statues in the churches, while Zwilling advised the faithful against attending Masses because these were a sin against the divine Majesty. The Augustinians, at their Chapter in Wittenberg, January 6, 1522, decreed that those who wished to leave the monastery might do so. Daily, private Masses were being discontinued and no liturgical services were taking their place.[15]

---

12 O'Donovan, *Assertio*, p. 269.

13 *Ibid.*, p. 275.

14 On Karlstadt, see the work of Ronald J. Sider, *Andreas Bodenstein von Karlstadt* (Leiden, 1974); and for Karlstadt's relations with Luther, see, by the same author as editor, *Karlstadt's Battle with Luther: Documents in a Liberal-Radical Debate* (Philadelphia, 1978), especially pp. 49–71, 147–59, for their different approaches to reform.

15 E. G. Schwiebert, *Luther and His Times* (St. Louis, 1950), pp. 536–38.

These were some of the developments which Luther witnessed on his return from the Wartburg. The pace of reform was too rapid, he thought. His first official effort to steer a middle course between these extreme measures and a reversion to the Roman Mass was an instruction to the Church of Leisnig, Saxony: *Von Ordnung Gottesdiensts in der Gemeine* (January 1523). In this very brief work, Luther recommended that a form of Matins and Vespers be held daily in the church. A selection from Scripture was to be read at these services, alternating between the Old and the New Testaments, followed by an explanation of the reading for those present (*WA* 12, 35–36; *LW* 53, 12–13). Daily Masses, therefore, were to be discontinued, for the word is more important than the Mass. If, however, someone desired the sacrament during the week, Mass might be celebrated. The whole congregation was to come together for Mass and Vespers on Sunday (*WA* 12, 37; *LW* 53, 13). What Luther understands here by "Mass" is not clear, because he had not as yet set down the order of his evangelical Mass.

Luther had to direct a word of caution in another direction at this time. The Bohemian Brethren of Prague found Luther's early works on the Eucharist congenial to their thinking.[16] A catechism published by them in 1520, and again in 1523, contained implications concerning the presence of Christ's body in the Eucharist and, specifically, the adoration of the sacrament; and these implications disturbed Luther (*WA* 11, 417–18; *LW* 36, 271). In April 1523, he addressed the Brethren directly in *Von Anbeten des Sakraments des heiligen Leichnams Christi* in order to correct their interpretation of his doctrine.

Luther's principal concern in this work is to defend his belief that the bread is the true body of Christ and the wine his true blood against the error of those who would maintain that the sacrament is only bread and wine such as people commonly eat and drink, or that its reception merely symbolizes one's incorporation in the spiritual body of Christ.

---

[16] The most relevant work here would perhaps be *De captivitate Babylonica*, and the section in which Luther treats of transubstantiation, the second "captivity" of the Eucharist. The Bohemians originated as a group of Utraquists (those who held that the laity, like the clergy, should communicate under the forms of both bread and wine), and were organized as a Church by Lukas of Prague. Their efforts to join the Lutherans were successful only in 1542, when they accepted justification by faith alone and the Real Presence, but retained their discipline of public and private confession of sins. Cf. F. L. Cross and E. A. Livingstone, *The Oxford Dictionary of the Christian Church* (2nd ed., London, 1974), pp. 184–85.

On the adoration of the sacrament, Luther takes an ambiguous position: we ought not to condemn nor accuse of heresy those who do not adore the sacrament; we ought not to condemn nor accuse of heresy those who adore the sacrament; Christ has neither condemned nor forbidden such adoration (WA 11, 448; LW 36, 295). In addition, Luther takes the opportunity to warn his readers of the error of the pope and his followers, namely, "that they have made of the sacrament a sacrifice and a good work and thereby have deceived everybody" (WA 11, 441; LW 36, 288). But the word of Christ, by which he instituted the sacrament, says nothing about a sacrifice or good work. And this word is the whole gospel. Just as we cannot make out of the gospel a sacrifice or a work, so we cannot make a sacrifice or a work out of this sacrament (WA 11, 442; LW 36, 288–89).

Luther hopes for a more understanding response from the Bohemians than he received from the Roman theologians:

> If my papist opponents had been able to permit the friendly pointing out of their mistakes and if they had not opposed me, in return, with wantonness and violence, this whole business would not have developed, and their authority and honor would probably still remain. But I expect much better things from you than I received from those fellows, because you are reasonable people (WA 11, 452; LW 36, 300).

Besides their hope for an amicable settlement with the Brethren, these words are significant for two reasons: first, Luther hints that, had he been treated differently than he was, his break with Rome might not have occurred; secondly, since that condition had not been fulfilled, he was in 1523 quite aware that such a break had taken place.

Pressure was still on Luther to issue some guidelines for the order of an evangelical Mass. Nicholas Hausmann (1478–1538), a friend of Luther and a leader of the Reformation in Zwickau since 1521, was the most insistent advocate, because the trend to more radical reform was strongest in that city (WA 12, 197).[17] In December 1523, Luther

---

[17]   Some of the Zwickau "prophets," as they were called, came to Wittenberg at the end of 1521 and began preaching sermons based on the Scriptures and their own inspiration of the Spirit. They confused the people, who could not tell whether they were of God or of the devil and Luther, after his return to Wittenberg, tried to moderate their influence. In doing so he alienated his friend Karlstadt who sympathized with them. In 1525, Luther directed a burning attack on this wing of the Reformation in *Wider die himmlischen Propheten.* Cf. Mark U. Edwards, Jr., *Luther and the False Brethren* (Stanford, CA., 1975), pp. 20–24, 34–59.

was able to meet the demand with the publication in Latin of his *Formula Missae et Communionis*. Although addressed to Hausmann, it carried the sub-title "pro Ecclesia Vuittembergensi," and was perhaps intended for any evangelical congregation.

Luther offers an apology for his delay, but not without giving his own reasons:

> I have used neither authority or pressure. Nor did I make any innovations. For I have been hesitant and fearful, partly because of the weak in faith, who cannot suddenly exchange an old and accustomed order of worship for a new and unusual one, and more so because of the fickle and fastidious spirits who rush in like unclean swine without faith or reason, and who delight only in novelty and tire of it as quickly, when it has worn off. Such people are a nuisance even in other affairs, but in spiritual affairs, they are absolutely unbearable (*WA* 12, 205; *LW* 53, 19).

A sense of humane action in Luther's approach to liturgical reform is evident here and it corrects any tendency to regard him as an iconoclast. At the same time, there is an expression of impatience with the radical reformers, who had already begun to be a source of irritation for him.

Luther's purpose in the *Formula Missae* appears quite modest: not to abolish the liturgical service of God completely—this has never been his intention—but to purify that which is now in use from accretions that have corrupted it and to bring out its evangelical character (*WA* 12, 206; *LW* 53, 20). Accordingly, he does not draw up a new service but simply takes the Roman Mass as a basis and recommends substantial changes. He approves the first part of the Mass through the Nicene Creed almost as it stands, and recommends only minor revisions, such as limiting the collect prayers to one.

The main target of Luther's attack, the principal accretion which must be discarded, is the Canon, "that abominable concoction drawn from everyone's sewer and cesspool" (*WA* 12, 207; *LW* 53, 21). Through this abomination the Mass has become a sacrifice.[18] Offertories and mercenary collections were added and the Mass began to be a priestly monopoly devouring the wealth of the whole world. Everything that smacks of sacrifice must be rooted out. The Offertory and

---

[18]   Cf. *supra*, note 9, p. 34.

the Canon, therefore, are to be eliminated. The words of institution, the words of life and salvation, having been rescued from the centre of the Canon ("imbedded . . . as the ark of the Lord once stood in the idol's temple next to Dagon"), are to be recited aloud following the Preface (*WA* 12, 211; *LW* 53, 26). The elimination of the Offertory and the Canon is the most drastic change Luther makes in the Mass of the Roman rite. He shifts the *Sanctus* to follow the words of institution rather than the Preface, thereby retaining an emphasis on the presence of Christ, but he leaves the rest of the Mass substantially unchanged (*WA* 12, 212; *LW* 53, 28).

With regard to matters not pertaining to the order of the Mass, Luther displays considerable flexibility. Private confession before Communion is neither necessary nor to be demanded; nevertheless it is useful and should not be despised (*WA* 12, 216; *LW* 53, 34). Communion under both kinds may be requested and should be so offered in compliance with the institution of Christ. In fact, communicants should become accustomed to receiving the sacrament in this manner (*WA* 12, 217; *LW* 53, 35). Private Masses, said by the minister alone in an empty room, are contrary, Luther maintains, to the Lord's Supper which presupposes the presence of guests to share it. Therefore, these should not be allowed in the Church except as a temporary concession for the sake of necessity or for the weak in faith (*WA* 12, 215; *LW* 53, 32). Such matters as these could be further discussed before final decisions were reached regarding them. For the present, Luther's main objective in the *Formula Missae* was achieved: the implementation in a practical way of his understanding of the Eucharist—the removal from the order of divine service of anything which stated or implied that the Mass is a sacrifice.

Once again, the Bohemian Brethren provided Luther with the occasion to express himself on the Eucharist. From the nature of the circumstances, however, his subject had more to do with the ministry required for the Eucharist, that is, the priesthood. Succeeding popes in the previous century had refused to appoint an archbishop to the see of Prague for the Bohemians and their forebears, the Utraquists.[19] As a result, the archbishopric was vacant from 1421 to 1560 and a consistory of elected administrators ruled the churches (*WA* 12, 160). The

---

[19] Cf. *supra*, note 16, p. 38.

Bohemians were not content with this situation and one of them, Gallus Cahera, visited Wittenberg and persuaded Luther that his church inclined to his views and would be receptive to his advice on an adequate ministry (*WA* 12, 162). Towards the end of 1523, Luther addressed their church body in a short treatise, *De instituendis ministris Ecclesiae*, which was published in 1524.

The ministry of the priesthood is associated with sacrifice, and in such a way that, were there no sacrifice, there would be no need for a priesthood. This reasoning underlies the presentation of Luther's argument to the Bohemians: contrary to the papist doctrine, there is no sacrifice in Christian worship; therefore, there is no necessity for an ordained priesthood. Scripture, Luther maintains, and especially the Epistle to the Hebrews, teaches us that Christ is the high priest who, alone and once and for all, by offering himself has taken away the sins of all people and accomplished their sanctification. Using some texts (for example, 10:10; 10:14) which he had passed over in his own Commentary on Hebrews, Luther shows that there cannot be any other sacrifice than that of Christ. By putting our trust in it, we are saved from sin without any merits or works of our own. A perpetual remembrance of this offering Christ has instituted to be proclaimed in the sacrament of the altar (*WA* 12, 175; *LW* 40, 14).

But the papists do not respect this one sacrifice of Christ. They offer his body and blood in innumerable places in the world, promising not an eternal but a daily remission of sins. Such an abomination goes beyond all reason:

> For if I believe that Christ, offered once for all, has won for me perpetual forgiveness of sins, I cannot seek forgiveness anew by some other sacrifice. For if I seek forgiveness by a daily sacrifice there is no room for a faith that the unique sacrifice of Christ has taken away all my sins forever (*WA* 12, 175; *LW* 40, 15).

Failure to accept the integral promise of Christ results in a weakening of faith which, as Luther has expressed often before, is accompanied by a corresponding emphasis on works.

As the New Testament speaks of no sacrifice except that of Christ, Luther's argument continues, so it speaks of no ordained priest:

> For a priest, especially in the New Testament, was not made but was born. He was created, not ordained. He was born not indeed of flesh,

but through a birth of the Spirit, by water and Spirit in the washing of regeneration (John 3:6ff.; Titus 3:5ff.). Indeed, all Christians are priests, and all priests are Christians (*WA* 12, 178; *LW* 40, 19).

Baptism, the sacrament that makes us Christians, also makes us priests. And we need no further power than that bestowed in this sacrament to function as priests. To illustrate this point, Luther next explains the different functions of a priest, indicating how each one comes within the competence of every Christian. Two functions are especially related to the Eucharist. One function, to consecrate and to administer the sacred bread and wine, belongs to all: the injunction of Christ at the Last Supper, "Do this in remembrance of me" (Lk. 22:19; I Cor. 11:24), was not to be claimed by a few special people as giving them the power to consecrate, but instead was extended to all those then present and to those who in the future would be present at the table (*WA* 12, 182; *LW* 40, 24). The other function, to sacrifice, likewise applies to all Christians: the only sacrifice required of us in the New Testament is that described by St. Paul in Rom. 12:1, which bids us present our bodies as a sacrifice, just as Christ sacrificed his body for us on the cross. In this sacrifice Paul includes the sacrifice of praise and thanksgiving. The "spiritual sacrifices" recommended in I Pet. 2:5 refer also to the sacrifice of ourselves (*WA* 12, 185; *LW* 40, 28–29). These functions, like the others, are within the competence of any Christian, as Luther makes clear in his summary statement:

> Here we take our stand: There is no other Word of God than that which is given all Christians to proclaim. There is no other baptism than the one which any Christian can bestow. There is no other remembrance of the Lord's Supper than that which any Christian can observe and which Christ has instituted. There is no other kind of sin than that which any Christian can bind or loose. There is no other sacrifice than the body of every Christian. No one but a Christian can pray. No one but a Christian may judge of doctrine. These make the priestly and royal office (*WA* 12, 189–90; *LW* 40, 34–35).

Since the Bohemians certainly considered themselves Christians, Luther's practical advice to them is almost predictable: because the papal bishops are unwilling to bestow the ministry of the word except on such as destroy the word and ruin the Church, let the Bohemians come together, cast ballots and elect one or as many as are needed for

the ministry from those who are capable. By prayer and the laying on
of hands, let them commend these to the whole assembly, and recognize
and honour them as lawful ministers of the word, believing beyond all
doubt that this has been done and accomplished by God (*WA* 12, 191;
LW 40, 37). In this way the Bohemians will have legitimate ministers
for their churches.

The scene changes back to Wittenberg from Prague for the compo-
sition of Luther's next work on the Mass, the last to be considered
in this chapter. Luther had advised his fellow Augustinians from the
Wartburg to cease saying Mass, except for the motive of faith (*WA* 8,
560; *LW* 36, 226). Even while trying to moderate Karlstadt's inno-
vations in the new evangelical Mass after his return to Wittenberg,
Luther continued to call for the abolition of the Roman Mass in his
lectures and sermons.[20] By the end of 1524, with the support of the
town council, the University of Wittenberg and the majority of the
citizens, Luther was successful in having the Mass discontinued at the
Castle Church.[21] To continue this campaign and to instruct the simple
and unlearned as well as the educated in his objections to the Mass,
Luther wrote *Vom Greuel der Stillmesse* in the early months of 1525. In
the Roman Mass, the Canon was recited silently by the celebrant. Luther, therefore, terms it "die Stillmesse,"[22] and, in this work, seeks to
show how it is an abomination by exposing the false doctrine expressed
in the prayers of the Canon. Since he had eliminated the Canon (except
for the words of institution) in his *Formula Missae*, the term "Stillmesse" would also clearly identify the Roman Mass as distinct from
the evangelical Mass.

Before commenting on certain prayers of the Canon, Luther situates
his ideas concerning the Eucharist within the wider context of salvation. The problem of salvation from sin, death and the devil, of
attaining true righteousness before God and eternal life, is one that
concerns all people. But it cannot be solved by works or laws. The only

---

[20] A sermon preached in Wittenberg on November 27, 1524, is thought to be the basis
of this present work, *Vom Greuel der Stillmesse*. Cf. *WA* 18, 12–13.
[21] Schwiebert, *Luther and His Times*, p. 544.
[22] I base this meaning of the term on the following words of Luther as he begins his
critique of the prayers of the Canon: "Nu wollen wyr die wort her zelen, so die pfaf-
fen ynn der stillmess heymlich lesen, Wilche sie den Canon nennen, und so trefflich
hoch heiligthum halten, das sie den selben den leyen verbieten zu wissen" (*WA* 18,
24).

means of solution is that which God has provided. There is no other mediator than his only Son, whom he sent into the world and whom he caused to shed his blood. There is no other mediation than this one sacrifice of Christ on the cross, whereby he put away the sins of all and made us holy for all eternity (*WA* 18, 23; *LW* 36, 312–13). To such a mediator, to such a mediation, we respond in faith. And if anyone seeks another way to be freed from his sins and stand before God, he blasphemes and insults God. He accuses him of lying, as if he had let his Son shed his blood in vain and his death had accomplished nothing (*WA* 18, 23; *LW* 36, 313).

But the papists have managed to find another way:

> In the Mass the papists do nothing but continually ride the words, "we offer up, we offer up" and "these sacrifices, these gifts." They keep completely quiet about the sacrifice that Christ has made. They do not thank him. Indeed, they despise and deny his sacrifice and try to come before God with their own sacrifice (*WA* 18, 24; *LW* 36, 313).

To substantiate this accusation, Luther now comments on the prayers of the Canon. For example:

"Therefore, most merciful Father, we humbly beg and entreat you through Jesus Christ your Son, our Lord, to accept and bless these gifts, these offerings, these holy and spotless sacrifices which we offer you . . . ."[23] The priest has before him a wafer of simple bread and a cup of wine; yet he regards these as a sacrifice before God on behalf of the whole Church. This is surely a blasphemy against Christ's own blood (*WA* 18, 25; *LW* 36, 314).

"Remember, O Lord, your servants N. and N., and all here present, whose faith and devotion are known to you. For whom we offer, or who themselves offer, to you this sacrifice of praise . . . for the redemption of their souls. . . ." Here are remembered those for whom the sacrifice is offered. The offering is for "the redemption of their souls." Yet the Canon prayer has just spoken of their "faith." If they have faith, why should their souls need redemption? (*WA* 18, 26; *LW* 36, 316).

---

[23] This translation of the prayers in the Roman Missal is from *The Maryknoll Missal* (New York: P. J. Kenedy & Sons, 1964), reflecting the wording of the Roman Canon before its revision following Vatican Council II.

"Take, all of you, and eat of this: For this is my Body." In these words of consecration, the papists omit the important words, "which is given for you" (Lk. 22:19). In this way, they remain silent about the sacrifice which Christ has made (WA 18, 28; LW 36, 319).
"We, your servants, O Lord, and with us your holy people . . . offer to your supreme majesty . . . a perfect, holy, and unblemished Victim. . . ." Christ offered himself only once (Heb. 9:25–26) and cannot die or be offered up again (Rom. 6:9–10). Yet here, the priests presume to offer him again; indeed, Christ is offered every day more than a hundred thousand times throughout the world (WA 18, 29; LW 36, 320).

From these examples it is clear that Luther regarded the Roman Mass as a sacrifice apart from the unique sacrifice of Christ. In his *Formula Missae*, he eliminated the Canon in order to preserve the evangelical Mass from the overtones of such a sacrifice. Here, in *Vom Greuel der Stillmesse*, Luther shows more specifically from his interpretation of the prayers of the Canon why he found it imperative to make this drastic excision.

If the period 1517–1520 was one in which Luther formulated his new theology of the Eucharist, the period 1521–1525 may be characterized as one in which he implemented this theology. The implementation was gradual; it began with Luther advising and persuading from his own convictions based on the Scriptures and proceeded to rather firm directives for abolishing the Roman Mass. Along the way, he considered related topics in his arguments, notably the act of atonement and the priesthood of all believers. The year 1525 does not mark the end of Luther's preoccupation with the Mass as sacrifice, nor the full accomplishment of his objective of providing an adequate substitute for it. But it could be said that his interest in the subject reaches a kind of plateau—at least for a few years, while other issues become the centre of his attention.

CHAPTER III
1526–1544

y 1525, Luther had to deal with the radical left wing of the Reformation movement. The most noted preacher of this group, called *Die Schwärmer*, was Thomas Münzer (1489–1525). He had been present at the Leipzig Debate in 1519, and was impressed with Luther's performance in his discussions with Eck, especially his appeal to Scripture as the solid basis of his arguments. Münzer later became a minister in Zwickau through Luther's influence and soon established himself as a man with a mission: under the inspiration of the Holy Spirit, he believed that he was commissioned to inaugurate the Kingdom of God on behalf of the elect, by force and social revolution if necessary. The churches were not receptive to his message, and he shifted from Zwickau to Prague, from Prague to Allstedt, and eventually became an itinerant preacher of his "gospel." Luther dissociated himself from Münzer's interpretation of the Scriptures in his *Brief an die Fürstin zu Sachsen von dem aufrührischen Geist* of 1524. Münzer himself became actively involved in the Peasants' Revolt. After their defeat at the battle of Frankenhausen, he was captured and executed.[1]

Reference has already been made to some of Luther's difficulties with Andreas Karlstadt, a more moderate spokesman of *Die Schwärmer*.[2] After leaving Wittenberg in 1522, Karlstadt became a layman, taking on the manner of life of the peasants, for he believed that it was from them, the simple people, that one could learn the meaning of Scripture.

---

[1]   Schwiebert, *Luther and His Times*, pp. 546–48.
[2]   Cf. *supra*, p. 37, and footnote 17, Chapter II, p. 39.

Like Münzer, he felt that he had a prophetic mission, but stopped short of preaching revolution and bloodshed. In his publications, he continued to oppose Luther on the doctrine of the Eucharist: Christ is not actually present in the sacrament, he taught; yet the sacrament is a commemoration of Christ's death. For a time Luther was patient with his former friend and associate, but then he roundly condemned him in the tract *Wider die himmlischen Propheten* of 1525.[3]

After the Peasants' Revolt was crushed, Karlstadt wandered as a preacher through southern Germany and eventually settled in Zurich, Switzerland. His ideas on the Eucharist found receptive soil in the city of Strassburg especially, and specifically with the leader of the reform movement there, Martin Bucer (1491–1551).[4] After an inconclusive attempt to obtain some clarification of the doctrine of the Eucharist from Luther, Bucer undertook his own examination of the pertinent passages in Scripture and concluded that the symbolic presence of Christ in the sacrament is the only tenable interpretation. The force of *est* in the formula of institution, *Hoc est corpus meum*, is *significat*. This interpretation was soon adopted also by leading reformers in other cities, for example, by Ulrich Zwingli (1484–1531) in Zurich and by John Oecolampadius (1482–1531) in Basle, and the stage was set for a bitter controversy between Luther and these reformers over the Real Presence of Christ in the Eucharist.[5] A "second front,"[6] consisting of theologians who likewise appealed to the Scriptures, though with differing conclusions, now engaged Luther's attention. For the purposes of this study, it is sufficient to observe that it is this controversy on the Real Presence that constitutes the principal background of Luther's works on the Eucharist in the period 1526–1530. Some of these writings—for the sake of a comprehensive study—will be examined for references to the Mass as sacrifice.

In his *Formula Missae* of 1523, Luther had retained the Latin language in the order of service, except for the sermon and hymns. Münzer, in the same year, celebrated the first public worship in German at

---

[3] Schwiebert, *Luther and His Times*, pp. 548–50.
[4] Bucer was also influenced by a book on the Eucharist written by a certain Christopher Honius of the Netherlands. In it, Honius argued for a position similar to Karlstadt's on the presence of Christ in the sacrament. Cf. Schwiebert, *Luther and His Times*, p. 697.
[5] Schwiebert, *Luther and His Times*, p. 697.
[6] Wisløff, *The Gift of Communion*, p. 3.

Allstedt.[7] As this practice became more widespread on the initiative
of individual pastors, the need for a German order of service as norm-
ative became apparent, and Luther was petitioned to produce one (*WA*
19, 45). He demanded some time to draw up this service, not wishing
merely to make a German translation, but also to provide music suit-
able to the German character and language for the sung Masses (*WA*
19, 46). In 1526, he issued *Deutsche Messe und Ordnung Gottesdiensts*.
While acknowledging the need for some degree of uniformity in
worship, Luther cautions his readers against making a fixed reg-
ulation out of the order of service he provides:

> In the first place, I would kindly and for God's sake request all those
> who see this order of service or desire to follow it: Do not make it a rigid
> law to bind or entangle anyone's conscience, but use it in Christian
> liberty as long, when, where, and how you find it to be practical and
> useful (*WA* 19, 72; *LW* 53, 61).

In this way, he guards against the basic defect of the papist services:
in these, the authorities have made laws, works, merits out of them,
so that the common people are not instructed in the word of God but
regard instead the services themselves as necessary for salvation (*WA*
19, 73; *LW* 53, 62). Luther recommends three basic services: the Latin
Service of the *Formula Missae*, which may be retained;[8] the German
Mass, which he details in this work; and a kind of unstructured service
for small groups that convene for prayer and the sacrament as part of
their sharing in apostolic works (*WA* 19, 73–75; *LW* 53, 62–64). These
options provide pastors with some choice even within Luther's directives.
Structurally, Luther introduced few changes in the German Mass. The
Canon, except for the words of institution, is omitted in accordance
with his previous directive in *Formula Missae*. A public paraphrase of
the Lord's Prayer follows upon the sermon and displaces the Preface,
which had served to introduce the institution of the sacrament (*WA*
19, 95–96; *LW* 53, 78–79). This re-arrangement of the Lord's Prayer

---

[7]   Lortz, *The Reformation*, I, p. 356.
[8]   Not only does Luther want the Latin Service retained, but if Hebrew and Greek were
      as well known as Latin and German, he would prefer that Masses be said or sung in all
      four languages on successive Sundays (*WA* 19, 74; *LW* 53, 63).

is the most significant change. In arranging the sung parts of the
Mass—the *Kyrie*, Epistle, Gospel and *Sanctus*—Luther was assisted by
two musicians of Elector Frederick's own chapel, Conrad Rupsch
(d. 1525) and Johann Walter (1496–1570) (*WA* 19, 48–49).

The sermon is a most important part of the service, no matter what
order or language is chosen. And here Luther shows less flexibility.
He suggests, in fact, that a *Kirchenpostille* be composed for the entire
year, with sermons to be read for each day in the manner of the homilies
that are read at Matins of the Divine Office. Such a sermon guide would
assist preachers who are unable to prepare well and, most especially,
would be a check on those who preach their own ideas and thus distort
and neglect the gospel (*WA* 19, 95; *LW* 53, 78). Unless the true gospel
is explained to the people, especially the words of institution—the
"sum of the gospel"—they will lose sight of what Luther has explicitly
mentioned in the paraphrase of the Lord's Prayer: that the faithful be
able to discern the testament of Christ in true faith and to attend to
the words wherein Christ imparts to them his body and his blood for
the remission of their sins (*WA* 19, 96; *LW* 53, 79–80).

Luther no doubt had *Die Schwärmer* in mind as "those who preach
their own ideas." Particularly painful to him were the interpretations
currently given to the words of institution, which affected not only the
sacrament as testament but also the presence of Christ in the sign of
the testament. At the urging of Landgrave Philip of Hesse (1504–
1567), one of Luther's ablest supporters among the German princes,
he undertook in 1527 a refutation of these interpretations with an
extensive treatise, *Dass diese Wort Christi "Das ist mein Leib" noch fest
stehen wider die Schwarmgeister*. It was directed principally against the
writings of Zwingli, Oecolampadius and Bucer. Thus, the term
Schwarmgeister in the title indicates a category of people rather than a
specific group, such as *Die Schwärmer*. The category includes those more
influenced by private revelation (supposedly under the Spirit but actually, according to Luther, under the devil) than by the word of God
in formulating their doctrine (*WA* 23, 65–67; *LW* 37, 13–14).

The treatise is almost exclusively concerned with how Christ is present
in the Eucharist, Luther arguing that he is present not just figu-
ratively, but really—not indeed a corporeal presence involving space
but a personal presence involving faith. At one point, however, Luther
feels sure that he will find his adversaries in agreement with him: in
rejecting the idea that the sacrament is also a sacrifice. Whether they

consider the sacrament nothing but bread or as Christ's body, they can be certain of one thing: that Christ is not sacrificed over and above the one single historical event in which he sacrificed himself. According to Luther, we may refer to the Eucharist as a sacrifice in the sense that we offer bread and wine, which become the sacrament through God's word, for the sole purpose of giving thanks, that we may thereby acknowledge how God nourishes us. But the purpose is not to redeem our souls or propitiate God, as the papists claim when they celebrate Mass. Again, Luther's argument continues, we may call the sacrament a sacrifice because by it we remember the one sacrifice Christ made for us, just as we remember his resurrection at Easter and say "Christ is risen today"—not that Christ rises every year but that every year we commemorate the day of his resurrection (*WA* 23, 273; *LW* 37, 144). We can go this far in speaking of the sacrament or the Mass as a sacrifice, but no further.

Following the pattern for controversy of the day, Luther's opponents, especially Zwingli and Oecolampadius, quickly replied to his treatise with tracts of their own (*WA* 26, 243). Copies of the tracts reached Luther in November 1527; in December he set to work on what he hoped would be his definitive statement on the disputed question, *Vom Abendmahl Christi, Bekenntnis*, which was published in February of the following year (*WA* 26, 245–46).[9] His objective is clear from his own brief outline of the treatise:

> Three things, however, I propose to do in this little book. First, to warn our people by showing that this fanatical spirit has completely failed to answer my arguments. Secondly, to analyse the scriptural passages which teach of the holy sacrament. Thirdly, to confess all the articles of my faith in opposition to this and every other new heresy, so that neither during my lifetime nor after my death will they be able to claim that Luther agreed with them—as they have already done in certain instances (*WA* 26, 262; *LW* 37, 163).

Again, Luther is primarily concerned with those who deny the Real Presence of Christ in the Eucharist; and yet, he makes some points in

---

9   That Luther's hopes were not in vain is indicated by the editor in assessing the importance of this work in the introduction: "In den Abendmahlstreitigkeiten späterer Jahrhunderte ist Luthers 'Grösses' Bekenntnis das Schiboleth der echten Lutheraner geblieben" (*WA* 26, 249).

this summary of his doctrine which are worthy of notice because they
pertain to the subject of this study.

In dealing with the passages of Scripture that refer to the Eucharist,
for example, Luther excludes any sacrificial interpretation for some
reasons not indicated in previous works. When St. Paul recounts the
institution of the sacrament, "This is my body which is broken for
you" (I Cor. 11:24), these words should be understood to refer simply
to the breaking and distributing of the sacrament at the table. By
inference, Luther argues, the same interpretation applies to the cup of
wine: the words "poured out for many," in the account in the Synoptics
(Matt. 26:28; Mk. 14:24), refer not to Christ's sacrifice on the cross
but to the distribution at table (WA 26, 470; LW 37, 328). Thus,
while concentrating on certain exegetical emphases vis-à-vis Die
Schwarmgeister, Luther does not neglect to assert his convictions on
another aspect of the Eucharist, that is, its non-sacrificial dimension.

Given his primary audience, one important emphasis for Luther is
the objective validity of the sacrament. The external components
of the sacrament point to its interior effects, and all are connected in
a single unity:

> The words are the first thing, for without the words the cup and the
> bread would be nothing. Further, without bread and cup, the body and
> blood of Christ would not be there. Without the body and blood of
> Christ, the new testament would not be there. Without the new testa-
> ment, forgiveness of sins would not be there. Without forgiveness of
> sins, life and salvation would not be there (WA 26, 478–79; LW 37,
> 338).

Although Luther here presupposes faith for the efficacy of the sacrament, in this description of its structure he exhibits a better balance
than in some of his earlier works,[10] where he was intent on emphasizing
faith over against the sacramental aspect of the Eucharist. Later in this

---

[10]   Cf., for example, his *Sermon von dem hochwürdigen Sakrament* . . . (WA 2, 751) in
       which Luther is strongly critical of the celebration of the Eucharist without regard for
       the manner in which it is celebrated or the dispositions of the celebrant; also, *De cap-
       tivitate Babylonica* (WA 6, 518), in which he quotes Augustine with approval, "Crede
       et manducasti." Luther's development in his understanding of the "sacrament" aspect
       of the Eucharist vis-à-vis the Augustinian model is carefully documented by Ralph
       W. Quere, "Changes and Constants: Structure in Luther's Understanding of the Real
       Presence in the 1520's," *The Sixteenth Century Journal* XVI (Spring 1985), 45–76.

treatise, in fact, he maintains that people receive the true body and blood of Christ even if those who distribute the sacrament do not believe in it. The sacrament does not depend upon one's belief or unbelief; it is God's word and ordinance that are important, provided these are not changed or misinterpreted (*WA* 26, 506; *LW* 37, 367). True, it is the faith of the minister rather than the communicant that is involved in this last reference, but the recognition of the objective validity of the sacrament is noteworthy.

Zwingli and Oecolampadius could not accept Luther's arguments for the Real Presence in his *Bekenntnis*, and the battle of the tracts continued. Although differences between the parties were freely aired at the Colloquy of Marburg in 1529 and agreement in some areas was indicated in the *Marburg Articles*, no accord was reached on this aspect of the Eucharist.[11] In 1530, another opportunity for airing differences, involving Catholic representatives as well, was provided at the Diet of Augsburg. This time the initiative came from Emperor Charles. Sensing the danger of Turkish invasion, he invited German princes, bishops and theologians to a hearing at Augsburg where their differences would be resolved and, as a united Christendom, the Empire could face the common enemy. Charles was somewhat naive in his objective; he had been absent from Germany for nine years, engaged in campaigns in Italy, and was perhaps not sufficiently aware that not even the reformers presented a united front at this time.[12]

As the hearing developed in practice, it consisted principally of submissions by the Lutheran and Catholic delegations. Elector John of Saxony (1468–1532), who had succeeded Frederick the Wise in 1525, was the acknowledged secular leader of the Lutheran representatives. Luther accompanied them as far as the Castle Coburg and took up residence there instead of venturing into Augsburg itself, since he was still technically under the ban of the Empire. From the Coburg, he could follow the proceedings and act as advisor.[13] Although considerable preparation had been given to a creedal statement, the task of making further revisions and drafting its final form fell to Luther's

---

[11] Cf. *LW* 38, 12–13, 85–89.
[12] Schwiebert, *Luther and His Times*, pp. 714–16.
[13] *Ibid.*, p. 720. Other prominent theologians in the Lutheran delegation were: Philipp Melanchthon (1497–1560), Georg Spalatin (1484–1545), Johann Agricola (c. 1494–1566) and Justus Jonas (1493–1555). Cf. *WA* 30[2], 237.

colleague, Philipp Melanchthon (1497–1560). It was presented to the Diet on June 25, 1530, as the *Confessio Augustana*.[14]

From his position "in the wings," Luther found it hard to keep out of the fray. Since he could not take part in the proceedings, he wrote an instruction to the participants: *Vermahnung an die Geistlichen, versammelt auf dem Reichstag zu Augsburg. Anno 1530.* He sent it to the publishers in May 1530 and it was available in Augsburg by June 12, two weeks before the *Confessio* was presented to the Diet.[15] In a way, the exhortation is Luther's own *Confessio*: as a review of the contribution of the Reformation to the Church, it seeks to gain the sympathetic ear of both prince and bishop.[16]

Since this is the nature of the document, Luther returns to the issue of the abuses in the Roman Church.[17] Concerning the Mass, he points out that it had become simply a matter of trade. Many thousands of Masses were bought and sold every day throughout the world. If money was not given, the Masses remained unsaid. In words calculated to catch the interest of Charles at least, Luther deplores such a crime:

> This sin alone is so terrible that it would be no wonder if God had let the whole world become Turks or sink into an abyss because of it. That God could tolerate it so long is one of the things at which I greatly wonder (*WA* 30[2], 293; *LW* 34, 22).

Even if money were not demanded for Masses, there remains the abuse that Masses are offered as a sacrifice and a good work, as satisfaction for sin, both for us and for others, for the living and especially for the dead. When Luther recalls how he was given this power by the bishop to offer sacrifice for the living and the dead, he reflects in apocalyptic vein: "That the earth did not swallow us both was unjust and due to God's all too great patience" (*WA* 30[2], 306; *LW* 34, 30).

---

[14] The document is included in the *Book of Concord*, trans. & ed., Theodore G. Tappert (Philadelphia, 1959), pp. 24–96.

[15] Justus Jonas refers to the work in a letter of this date, *WABr* 5, 358.

[16] Lorenzo Campeggio (1472–1539), papal legate and leader of the Catholic representation at the Diet, had it translated into Latin. The translator, Daniel Mauch, wrote of it to a friend: "Est autem summa totius Lutheranismi. Si totum Lutherum videre vis, emere poteris . . . " (*WA* 30[2], 238).

[17] For such abuses, including those of the pre-Reformation Church, cf. Jared Wicks, "Abuses Under Indictment at Augsburg," *Theological Studies* XLI (June 1980), 253–302.

Another related abuse of the Mass, Luther continues, has been the practice of the private Masses. From the earliest days of the Church, the Canons presuppose the communion of the faithful. But in private Masses, offered usually for the souls of the dead, the faithful do not receive communion; only the priest communicates. In this way, the sacrifice-aspect of the Mass is emphasized (following the imitation of Old Testament practice in the early Church) to the exclusion of the communion-aspect. The comparison between private Masses and those at which the faithful communicate is like that between a priest's secret mistress and an honest, acknowledged wife (WA 30[2], 294–95; LW 34, 23)!

In like manner, Luther discusses other doctrinal points, which are not pertinent here. The tone of the exhortation is generally not very conciliatory.[18] In this respect, it contrasts with the moderate exposition of Melanchthon's *Confessio*. Although Luther approved successive revisions of the document, he eventually felt that Melanchthon had passed over some points of difference too lightly.[19] Even at this, Melanchthon's effort contributed little to a reconciliation at the Diet. After study of the *Confessio*, a Catholic response was prepared by a group of theologians directed by the papal legate, Lorenzo Campeggio (1472–1539), and was presented to the Diet as the *Confutatio Pontificia*. Emperor Charles considered the issue settled. He granted to the signees of the *Confessio* a period of grace lasting to the following April, at which time they

---

[18] In treating of Communion under both kinds, for example, Luther declares: "Wo es Gott schickt, das yhr ettwas nach lasset auff diesem Reichstage, so wollen wirs nicht der meinung von euch annemen, als sey es durch ewr nachlassen nu recht, und bis her unrecht gewesen. . . . Sondern wir wollens euch durch Gotts wortt abgezwungen . . ." (WA 30[2], 322). In ecumenical discussions of recent years, the proposal has been made that the Catholic Church accept the *Confessio Augustana* as a creedal document. For this discussion, cf. Joseph A. Burgess, ed., *The Role of the Augsburg Confession: Catholic and Lutheran Views* (Philadelphia, 1980). The *Confessio* was prominent in the Lutheran–Roman Catholic discussions in Germany, 1976–1982; cf. Karl Lehmann and Edmund Schlink, eds., *Das Opfer Jesu Christi und seine Gegenwart in der Kirche*, especially the papers by Erwin Iserloh and Wolf-Dieter Hauschild, pp. 96–137.

[19] Schwiebert, *Luther and His Times*, pp. 728, 730. Melanchthon was prepared to retain the power of the bishops, provided the gospel was preached in their jurisdictions, and he omitted from the *Confessio* any refutation of the primacy of the pope. Instead, he concentrated on such points of difference as the marriage of priests, both forms in the sacrament, the Mass, the property of the Church. Cf., further, Lortz, *The Reformation*, II, pp. 6off.

would be expected to confess the articles of the *Confutatio* with the other Christian princes and bishops until eventually a general council could be convoked.[20] Another impasse in understanding had been reached and would continue unresolved.

During his stay in the Castle Coburg, Luther wrote another exhortation, *Vermahnung zum Sakrament des Leibes und Blutes Christi* (1530). Although its addressees are not clearly indicated,[21] it seems to be principally a continuation of Luther's dialogue with the Zwinglians. Its interest for this study is that, in the course of the exhortation, Luther re-enforces an important point, which he made in his earlier works: that the notion of sacrifice must be kept entirely separate from the sacrament.[22] As a memorial of Christ's atoning work, the sacrament may be considered an offering of thanksgiving: " . . . for by this very remembrance we confess and thank God that we have been saved and become righteous and blessed by sheer grace through Christ's suffering" (*WA* 30[2], 610; *LW* 38, 117). In this sense the sacrament is *ein Danck-opffer*.

As Luther sees it, the danger in this concession is that the sacrament may become *ein Werckopffer*, as it has for the papists in the Mass:

> They made the sacrament which they should accept from God, namely, the body and blood of Christ, into a sacrifice and have offered it to the selfsame God. . . . Furthermore, they do not regard Christ's body and blood as a sacrifice of thanksgiving but as a sacrifice of works in which they do not thank God for his grace but obtain merits for themselves and others and, first and foremost, secure grace (*WA* 30[2], 610; *LW* 38, 117).

This shift in the understanding of the sacrament ultimately destroys it, therefore, even as a sacrifice of thanksgiving. For this reason, Luther prefers that the thanksgiving element of sacrifice be associated only with the use and reception of the sacrament rather than with the sacrament itself.

---

[20]   Schwiebert, *Luther and His Times*, pp. 731–34.

[21]   The editor of the Weimar text does not mention in the introduction (*WA* 30[2], 589–90) the occasion for the exhortation or those to whom it is directed; he merely establishes the time and place of writing.

[22]   Cf. *Ein Sermon von dem neuen Testament* (*WA* 6, 365); *De captivitate Babylonica* (*WA* 6, 524–25).

So far in his controversy with the Roman Church concerning the Eucharist, Luther has made only passing references to the practice of private Masses.[23] After 1530, this practice, as one of the chief abuses of the Mass, comes under fire from the reformer. It furnishes the subject matter for two treatises as he gains some respite from his encounters with the other reformers on the doctrine of the Real Presence and resumes his opposition to the Mass as sacrifice.

Particular circumstances prompted the first treatise, *Von der Winkelmesse und Pfaffenweihe* (1533). In his opening words, Luther alludes to the readiness of his representatives under Melanchthon at Augsburg to acknowledge the power of the bishops and even to be consecrated ministers by them, provided that they be free to preach the gospel. Since this condition was not fulfilled, but instead they were required to compromise the truth of the gospel, Luther wishes to register his evaluation of their consecration with chrism (*WA* 38, 171, 195). As a political consideration, Prince John of Anhalt (1513–1571), a supporter of Luther, was under pressure at the time from Catholic neighbours of the province to tolerate the celebration of Masses as in former times. A word from Luther on the subject would strengthen the hand of the prince in this issue (*WA* 38, 172–73).

As the title of the treatise suggests, it is a critique of both the private Mass and the sacrament of ordination to the priesthood. The logic of Luther's argument runs as follows: he first questions the validity of the private Mass, as to whether the sacrament is effected at all in its celebration;[24] then, since his conclusion is negative, he also considers of no validity the ordination of priests to celebrate private Masses as their main function (so-called "Mass-priests"). Unfortunately, Luther does not give any definition of "Winkelmesse" ("Corner Mass"), but from his treatment of it we may say he is referring to a Mass offered by a priest, in silence and often alone, usually for the deceased, and in which he alone communicates.

---

[23] In *De captivitate Babylonica*, he did not make much of the differences between the private and the public Mass, except that in the former, the priest alone communicates (*WA* 6, 525); in the *Formula Missae* he does not forbid private Masses outright, but allows them to continue for the time being, for the sake of some necessity or for the weak in faith (*WA* 12, 215).

[24] In some Latin outlines preparatory to the writing of the treatise, there were two questions that occupied Luther: (1) Quid, si papisticus pastor solum panem et vinum accipiat? (2) Quaeritur . . . an illi . . . habeant verum sacramentum? (*WA* 38, 175–76).

At the beginning of the treatise, Luther uses a clever literary device, which the commentators refer to as the *Teufelsdisputation*, to present his arguments: the devil himself taunts Luther about his previous Mass-practice and he tries, rather unconvincingly, to respond as a loyal friar. The main issue is raised in the opening scene of this little drama, as Luther describes it:

> Once I awakened at midnight and the devil began the following disputation with me in my heart . . . : "Listen, you very learned fellow, do you know that you said private masses for fifteen years almost daily? Did you not in reality commit sheer idolatry with such a mass and did you not worship there simply bread and wine, rather than Christ's body and blood, and enjoin others to worship them?" I reply: "But I am a consecrated cleric; I have received chrism and consecration from the bishop, and, in addition, have done all this because of the command to do so and in obedience to it. Why have I not performed the consecration validly, since I have spoken the words in earnest and said mass with all possible devotion? You certainly know this" (*WA* 38, 197; *LW* 38, 149–50).

The devil is not impressed; the Turks and the heathen follow the letter of their prescriptions with studied obedience and yet their religion is false.

The devil now substantiates his position with a number of arguments. Luther's faith has been basically misplaced. Instead of trusting in Christ as his Saviour, he has put his faith in the power to consecrate and to celebrate the Mass (*WA* 38, 198; *LW* 38, 150–51). This power to consecrate is contrary, moreover, to the mind of Christ. He intended that we should celebrate the sacrament in order that it might be shared with Christians and benefit them. The very word "communion" means fellowship. But in the *Winkelmesse*, Luther has received the sacrament alone and has not shared it with others. Was this the purpose of his consecration (*WA* 38, 198–99; *LW* 38, 151)? It was also the mind of Christ that, through the celebration of the sacrament, his death would be publicly proclaimed (I Cor. 11:26). But Luther has not done this in the private Mass: alone, he has whispered to himself; alone, he has received the sacrament (*WA* 38, 199; *LW* 38, 151). Again, the sacrament was intended for the community, to strengthen Christians who share it. But in the private Mass, Luther has reversed this intention: instead of being a sacrament-priest, he has become a sacrifice-priest, offering as an individual sacrifice to God what was meant as food for others. He has made of it a special work, not to be shared with others unless sold to them for a price (*WA* 38, 199; *LW* 38, 152). Under the welter of such arguments, Luther must surely question his priestly consecration: "But if you have been consecrated in opposition to Christ's intention, then your consecration is certainly false, anti-Christian, and altogether meaningless" (*WA* 38, 199; *LW* 38, 152).

L uther does not reply to these arguments separately but offers the general defence that he has celebrated these Masses according to the faith and intention of the Church, and surely this justifies them. Here, the devil finds him particularly vulnerable. The intention of the Church must derive from the word of God; and if one derives from God's word the intention of the Church concerning works, it is all the more important to derive from the same source the intention of the Church concerning points of doctrine. Only recourse to God's word will settle the issue. But this solution situates Luther in the web of despair, for the private Mass is itself a denial of that word from which one understands the institution of the sacrament (*WA* 38, 202–203; *LW* 38, 155–56).

H aving exposed the main defects of the private Mass in this little exchange with the devil, Luther carries on the discussion of the topic by question and answer. What about our ancestors who have attended private Masses in the past? We may simply commend them to the judgement of God, confident that he will extend leniency to them, as he did to the children of Korah (Num. 26:11). For us at the present time, however, who have come to understand the abomination of such Masses, there is time to desist and flee "with Lot out of this Sodom" (*WA* 38, 209; *LW* 38, 162). What about conscientious Masspriests? They may do as they please, according to Luther; but they will find no support for their practice in any injunctions of Christ (*WA* 38, 209; *LW* 38, 163). May the ordinary Christian fall back on his simple faith and thereby derive some benefit from private Masses, if he should be present at them? Hardly, because he cannot hear the words of the priest which would elicit his faith; therefore, he may only guess what the priest says (and what he believes) as he says the words of consecration (*WA* 38, 210; *LW* 38, 164–65). Does not the Mass-priest, in offering a private Mass, nevertheless act as a public figure, much like a notary, thus making his offering a public act? The priests themselves disclaim this, calling the Mass *missa privata*, indicating that the cleric is not a public person, like a notary, but a private one (*WA* 38, 211; *LW* 38, 165).

Luther now involves himself more personally in the discussion by recording his own experience of the celebration of private Masses in Rome during his visit to the city in 1511.[25] It is painful for him even to recall the experience:

> I was in Rome (for a short time), where I said so many masses and saw so many masses said, that I shudder when I think of it. There I heard among other clever and coarse anecdotes at mealtime courtiers laugh and boast about how some said mass and in connection with the bread and wine spoke these words: "Panis es, panis manebis; vinum es, vinum manebis" ["Bread you are, bread you shall remain; wine you are, wine you shall remain"]; and with these words they elevated [the host and wine for consecration]. Now I was a young and particularly earnest, devout monk who was offended by such words. What was I to think? . . . . What if they all, pope and cardinals, including the courtiers, said mass in this way? . . . . Besides, it also disgusted me very much that they could say mass so confidently and efficiently and in such haste as if they were engaged in juggling. For before I got to the gospel, the cleric next to me had concluded his mass, and they called aloud to me: Passa, passa—"Get going, hurry up," etc. (*WA* 38, 211–12; *LW* 38, 166).

For these abuses—the carnival atmosphere, the improper formulas, the speed with which the Masses are said—no simple solution is at hand. As Luther has learned in the *Disputation*, one cannot appeal to the intention of the Church with the plea that, since she cannot err, whatever is done in her name is correct (*WA* 38, 215; *LW* 38, 170–71). There are two kinds of intention of the Church in administering a sacrament, one grounded in the words of Scripture, the other the product of human minds. On this latter kind, Luther claims, is based the practice of *Winkelmessen* and the consecration of priests to offer them (*WA* 38, 216–17; *LW* 38, 172–73).

Yet upon this foundation a special class of *Winkelpfaffen* grew up in the Church. They were not true priests. They did not preach, baptize or absolve. They did not pray, except to mumble the words of the Psalter. They did not attend to the needs of the dying. They did not

---

[25]   Cf. Schwiebert, *Luther and His Times*, pp. 181ff.

communicate the sacrament but manipulated it as a sacrifice and good work for a price (*WA* 38, 222; *LW* 38, 179).

Luther was aware of these abuses of the word and the sacrament when he set about reforming the ministry and the rite of celebration and, in the last part of his treatise, he indicates how he attempted to eliminate them.

The sacrament of baptism enables one to administer the Eucharist. There is no need for a consecration with chrism to establish a higher, priestly state above that of the baptized (*WA* 38, 227; *LW* 38, 185). If any ordination rite is performed, this is no more than the recognition of the candidate's call to the office of ministry, the *Pfarrampt* (*WA* 38, 230; *LW* 38, 188). This foundation for the ministry is based on the word of God. And the word of God, "pure and certain," as Luther has discovered it, is of pivotal importance for the whole Church structure: "Where God's word is pure and certain, there everything else must be: God's kingdom, Christ's kingdom, the Holy Spirit, baptism, the sacrament (of the Lord's Supper), the office of the ministry, the office of preaching, faith, love, the cross, life and salvation, and everything the church should have" (*WA* 38, 237; *LW* 38, 196). It is the word of God that effects the sacrament, not anything one says or does, much less any power of consecration from chrism; it effects the sacrament according to the command and institution of Christ, who assured us (I Cor. 11:23ff.) that when we come together and say his words over the bread and wine, they become his body and blood (*WA* 38, 240; *LW* 38, 199).

Faithful attention, then, to God's word assures the proper ministry and the true sacrament. Luther draws together the elements of both in the portrait he gives of the true Lutheran Mass:

> There our pastor, bishop, or minister in the pastoral office, rightly and honorably and publicly called, having been previously consecrated, anointed and born in baptism as a priest of Christ, without regard to the private chrism, goes before the altar. Publicly and plainly he sings what Christ has ordained and instituted in the Lord's Supper. He takes the bread and wine, gives thanks, distributes and gives them to the rest of us who are there and want to receive them, on the strength of the words of Christ: "This is my body, this is my blood. Do this," etc. Particularly we who want to receive the sacrament kneel beside, behind and around him . . . all of us true, holy priests, sanctified by Christ's blood, anointed by the Holy Spirit, and consecrated in baptism. . . .

> We let our pastor say what Christ has ordained, not for himself as though
> it were for his person, but he is the mouth for all of us and we all speak
> the words with him from the heart and in faith, directed to the Lamb
> of God who is present for us and among us, and who according to his
> ordinance nourishes us with his body and blood. This is our mass, and
> it is the true mass which is not lacking among us (*WA* 38, 247; *LW* 38,
> 208–209).

In contrast is Luther's portrait of the private Mass of the papists, which
merits quotation as well:

> Now the papists . . . celebrate mass not only in disobedience to God
> but also, by blaspheming his ordinance and command, do not administer
> the sacrament to anybody, retain it for themselves alone and, besides,
> cannot be certain whether they are taking mere bread and wine or the
> body of Christ, because they do not enact it according to Christ's ordi-
> nance but according to their own ordinance contrary to Christ's ordi-
> nance. Also, no one can be sure whether they speak the words [of insti-
> tution] or not. Therefore no one can be obliged to believe their secret
> whispering. Consequently, they also do not preach anything to anyone,
> as Christ nevertheless commanded. . . . And finally, beyond such abom-
> inations and desecrations, it is their sublimest worship that they sacrifice
> this sacrament to God . . . and give and sell it to other Christians for
> money (*WA* 38, 249–50; *LW* 38, 210).

Luther is grateful to God that he has been able to dissociate himself
from the distortions of this last portrait, to which he for some time
contributed, and to know the true Christian Mass and the proper use
of the sacrament (*WA* 38, 249; *LW* 38, 209).

Among Luther's earliest theological works was his *Dictata super Psalterium* (1513–1516). Later in his career, as he lectured and preached
on the Psalms, he published more extensive commentaries on some of
them. Psalm 110 on kingship, lending itself easily to a Christian interpretation, was one of his favourites. In 1535, he gave a series of sermons
on it and these were collected and published the same year.[26] Of interest
here is his exposition of verse 4: "The Lord has sworn and will not
change his mind, / 'You are a priest forever after the order of Melchi-

---

[26]   The title of the work is *Der CX Psalm, Gepredigt und ausgelegt durch D. Mart. Luth.* in
WA 41, 79–239.

zedek.'" This verse gave Luther the opportunity to express from a different angle his maturing ideas on sacrifice and priesthood.

There is an allusion in the verse to Melchizedek, King of Salem, who, bearing bread and wine, went out to meet Abraham returning victorious from war (Gen. 14:18). Luther interprets this event to mean simply that Melchizedek brought food and drink with him and offered them to Abraham and his troops.[27] Similarly, Christ instituted the sacrament of his body and blood as bread and wine in order that Christians should come together to eat and drink of it—but not to sacrifice it (*WA* 41, 180; *LW* 13, 313). To use the sacrament as a sacrifice is the work of the Roman clerics, who presume to offer daily that sacrifice by which forgiveness of sin was obtained for all Christendom. "It is as though Christ had not done this very thing on the cross, as though his sacrifice had no validity and were of no value" (*WA* 41, 181; *LW* 13, 314).

Melchizedek was a priest as well as a king, and in this respect he prefigured Christ who offered this unique sacrifice for all humanity. Scripture describes a priest as a person whom God has ordained and commanded to mediate between God and his people. That is, a priest comes from God and brings us his word and doctrine; again, he presents himself to God to offer sacrifice and pray for us. The priestly office consists, then, of three functions: to teach or preach God's word, to sacrifice and to pray (*WA* 41, 183; *LW* 13, 315). The sacrificial function, as Luther has already made clear, is restricted to the person of Christ: he alone is the High Priest who has sacrificed himself for our sins that we might be reconciled to God. The functions of teaching and preaching God's word (provided it be preaching not just the law, but the gospel, that is, forgiveness) and of praying may be shared with others. With respect to the function of praying, Luther gives a significant description of Christ's continuing role as intercessor: since, despite his unique sacrifice, we are still sinful and spiritually weak, he must unceasingly represent us before the Father and intercede for us, that such weakness and sin not be counted to us, but that he may grant

---

27 Luther's interpretation here would not be far from contemporary exegesis of the passage: Eugene H. Maly, in *The Jerome Biblical Commentary* (Englewood Cliffs, N.J., 1968), p. 19, has "The mention of bread and wine may indicate a covenant meal." Cf., also, Myles M. Bourke in the same *Commentary*, p 393, with reference to Heb. 7:7.

us instead the strength and power of the Holy Spirit to overcome them (*WA* 41, 191; *LW* 13, 320). He goes on to supplement these ideas on the priesthood with his doctrine of the priesthood of all Christians and the office of the priesthood in the Church, emphasizing mainly the same aspects already noted, especially in the analysis of *Vom Missbrauch der Messe.*

Luther's second work on the private Mass grew out of a public disputation on the subject in Wittenberg sometime in the early months of 1536. A delegation of theologians from England, representing Henry VIII, was present (*WA* 39[1], 134). Of Luther's followers, Melanchthon, John Bugenhagen (1485–1558)[28] and Caspar Cruciger (1504–1548)[29] were among those who proposed arguments in "defence" of the private Mass. If one were to reconstruct the disputation from the account given (compiled perhaps by a secretary) it would seem that Luther first presented some arguments against the private Mass and then answered arguments proposed in its support. The account was published in the same year under the title *Die Disputation contra missam privatam.*

For some of his arguments, Luther relies on his previous work, *Von der Winkelmesse*, and a subsequent letter.[30] But he also introduces some new arguments to bolster his case. For example, his first argument is an historical one. The private Mass did not exist at the time of Augustine and Jerome. It was introduced by Gregory the Great (pope, 590–604). The Fathers before him spoke of a *missa publica* in which there was communication of the sacrament. But the figurative language with which they spoke of participation in such a Mass (referring to it as a spiritual, not a real, offering) led to ambiguous interpretation and the error of the papists in attributing to them the practice of the private Mass (*WA* 39[1], 141).

---

[28] In early life, Bugenhagen was a Premonstratensian canon of Treptow in Pomerania. After his marriage in 1522, Luther secured his appointment as pastor in Wittenberg in 1523, where he remained until his death. He was Luther's confessor and, among other services, assisted him in translating the Bible. Cf. Cross and Livingstone, *The Oxford Dictionary of the Christian Church*, 2nd ed., pp. 207–208.

[29] Professor at the University of Wittenberg and preacher at the Castle Church from 1528, he supported Luther in the work of reform but in his later life leaned more to Calvin's doctrine than to Luther's. Cf. *Lexikon für Theologie und Kirche* III, col. 101.

[30] *Ein Brief D. Martin Luthers von seinem Buch der Winkelmessen* (1534). Addressed to "a good friend," most likely Nicholas Hausmann, this letter was intended to allay the concern of Prince John of Anhalt that some parts of this previous work could be given a Zwinglian interpretation (*WA* 38, 257ff.).

Considering the private Mass as a current practice, Luther, with a bow to some participants and not a little irony, shows its invalidity in scholastic terms: "In the private mass, there is no efficient, formal or final cause of the sacrament. Therefore, there is no sacrament" (*WA* 39[1], 142).[31] Then he dutifully supports his argument with a contrasting statement for each part:

> The efficient cause is that Christ instituted the sacrament, not that one person alone benefit from it, but the whole church or (at least) many people. . . . The formal cause is the institution itself by Christ so that we receive the sacrament of the altar for the remission of sins. But the papists make it a sacrifice which avails *ex opere operato* for the living and the dead. The final cause is announcing the death of the Lord until he comes again. . . . But how, in the private mass, can the celebrant announce the death of the Lord when he announces it to himself, does not communicate others but feeds himself? (*WA* 39[1], 142–43).

Although Luther does not use the terms very accurately (all causes tend to be species of final cause), nevertheless they provide him with a different form in which to summarize his arguments against the private Mass. It should be noted, besides, that in arguing the final cause, he implies that the death of Christ is proclaimed not only in preaching the word but in the act of communicating as well.

Luther appeals again to his personal experience as a principal reason for his opposition to private Masses. While depicting the Mass-practice in Rome once more,[32] he tries to analyse the source of his anguish in celebrating Mass:

> Indeed, as often as I approached the altar to celebrate, I shuddered as if I were about to commit a great crime; and yet I did not know what it was that tormented my conscience. But it was the blasphemy of God because they were crucifying again my Lord. You young people do not know those horrors of conscience and the magnitude of the blasphemy. But we experienced them. Praise and glory to God who snatched us from this evil (*WA* 39[1], 150).

---

[31] I am not aware of an English translation of this work; this, and other quotations, are my own translation.

[32] "Vidi ego Romae in una hora et in uno altari Sancti Sebastiani septem missas celebrari" (*WA* 39[1], 150).

The private Mass, like any other Mass, presumes to be a sacrifice. It seemed to Luther, then, that he was sacrificing Christ anew in each Mass and this was nothing short of blasphemy.

But would it be possible to strip the private Mass of its abuses and still retain it? This is the suggestion of Melanchthon. Let the private Mass be offered according to the institution of Christ, not for any stipend money, not applied to any individual living or dead, but solely to recall the memory of Christ's passion and to celebrate the sacrament (WA 39[1], 155). No, not even such a "purified" private Mass would be acceptable to Luther. It would still not be according to the institution of Christ, which presumes that others are present to receive the sacrament. Moreover, there is no necessity to offer Mass in such a manner: if a person wishes to celebrate, why should he not receive the sacrament from another? Finally, there would still be the danger of abuses (WA 39[1], 155–56).

John Bugenhagen argues that the private Mass was in vogue even in apostolic times, citing as evidence that the Apostle Thomas offered a private Mass just before his martyrdom. What was practised in apostolic times and preserved by the Church should not be discarded now. In reply, Luther makes light of historical evidence of that kind: "Most of the accounts of the saints are so fictitious that you can scarcely find anything reliable in them" (WA 39[1], 160–61). He does not cite the origin of the private Mass with Pope Gregory as an argument here.

Another participant in the debate maintains that the essential parts of a sacrament are contained in a private Mass: *elementum*, the bread and wine, *verbum*, the words of Christ, not of the celebrant, effecting the sacrament, and *mandatum*, the injunction of Christ to celebrate the sacrament in his name. But the private Mass does not measure up to Luther's criterion on any of these points:

> The papists are not satisfied with the institution of Christ using bread and wine, but add a third element, namely, water. Secondly, they also add to the words of Christ many other words which are clearly contrary to his institution. Thirdly, in direct opposition to the injunction of Christ, they apply [the sacrament] to benefit others (WA 39[1], 168).

Since some of these objections may be made against the public Mass of the Roman rite as well, there is more than a hint here (and in his other arguments) that Luther's reasons for rejecting the private Mass, in its essentials, would be fundamentally the same as his reasons for rejecting the public Mass, that is, that it is considered as sacrificing Christ anew, and is used as a good work to obtain God's favour for others. In its practice, as a particular kind of abuse of the Mass, Luther sees it as an innovation of human tradition. These are the conclusions that may be drawn from his treatment of the private Mass in this debate.

Die Disputation contra missam privatam was to be Luther's last work dealing principally with the subject of the Mass. But his convictions concerning it did not waver in the years before his death in 1546, and he occasionally expressed them in unmistakable terms, especially in two confessional documents. The first of these is *Die Schmalkaldischen Artikel* (1537–1538). In 1536, the Elector John Frederick of Saxony (d. 1554) requested Luther to draw up a statement of the articles of the Lutheran faith, indicating where concessions could or could not be made to the Roman Church; this statement was to be proposed at the general council, which was to convene at Mantua in 1537 (*WA* 50, 165). After it was drawn up, John Frederick wished to have it approved by the princes and theologians of the Smalkald League,[33] hence its official title. Luther completed his assignment towards the end of 1536 and submitted the articles for review by a group of Wittenberg theologians (*WA* 50, 173). Illness prevented Luther from sponsoring them personally (*WA* 50, 175), but they were presented to the Smalkald Assembly in February 1537. Although not officially approved by the princes and theologians present,[34] they constitute a significant statement of Lutheran theology.[35]

Luther's position on the Mass is stated in the second part of the document containing those articles about which no discussion is admissible; these are the articles which pertain to the office and work of

---

[33] An alliance formed at Smalkalden, February 27, 1531, between the Protestant groups in Germany, in self-defence against Charles V, following his declaration at the Augsburg Colloquy of a period of grace, during which the Protestants were expected to subscribe to the *Confutatio* statement. Cf. Cross and Livingstone, *The Oxford Dictionary of the Christian Church*, 2nd ed., p. 1244.

[34] Forty-three theologians signed the Articles privately. Cf. Thomas M. McDonough, *The Law and the Gospel in Luther: A Study of Martin Luther's Confessional Writings* (Oxford, 1963), pp. 130–32, for a good summary of the background for the writing and approval of the Articles.

[35] An indication of the importance of the Articles is given by Luther himself in the Preface: "So hab ich gleich wol diese Artickel inn des wollen durch offentlichen druck an den tag geben, . . . damit die, so nach mir leben und bleiben werden, mein zeugnis und bekenntnis haben vorzuwenden, . . . darauff ich auch noch bisher bleiben bin und bleiben wil, mit Gottes gnaden" (*WA* 50, 193–94).

Christ, and our redemption. The first article affirms that Jesus Christ was put to death for our transgressions and raised for our justification, that it is he alone, upon whom God has laid the iniquities of us all, who takes away our sins and justifies us with his grace (*WA* 50, 198–99). The Mass-doctrine contradicts this article:

> The Mass in the papacy must be regarded as the greatest and most horrible abomination because it runs into direct and violent conflict with this fundamental article. Yet, above and beyond all others, it has been the supreme and most precious of the papal idolatries, for it is held that this sacrifice or work of the Mass (even when offered by an evil scoundrel) delivers men from their sins, both here in this life and yonder in purgatory, although in reality this can and must be done by the Lamb of God alone. . . . There is to be no concession or compromise on this article either, for the first article does not permit it (*WA* 50, 200).[36]

This is a strong statement of difference concerning a fundamental point in the Christian life: how the grace of Christ is mediated. Luther predicted that the discussion of the Mass (along with other practices in its wake, such as pilgrimages, fraternities, indulgences) would be the decisive issue of the council. He knew the Roman position would be inflexible: Campeggio had said at Augsburg that he would rather be torn apart than give up the Mass. For his part, Luther declared in advance that he would rather be burned to ashes than acknowledge a celebrant of the Mass as equal or superior to his Saviour, Jesus Christ (*WA* 50, 204).

The general council did not convene at Mantua in 1537. It finally convened at Trent in December 1545—just two months before Luther's death. His preparatory work in *Die Schmalkaldischen Artikel* was never presented on the floor of the council, but it stood as his firm position on the doctrine of the Mass until his death. As late as 1544, he reviewed his long-standing opposition to the Mass in *Kurzes Bekenntnis vom heiligen Sacrament*, in the context of the elevation of the Host:

> Twenty or twenty-two years ago when I began to condemn the mass and wrote sharply against the papists that it was not a sacrifice or our work but a gift and present or a testament from God, which we could not

---

[36]   Translation is from the *Book of Concord*, p. 293.

sacrifice to God but which we should and had to receive from God, even
as baptism was not a sacrifice but a gracious gift of God, etc., at that
time I was indeed inclined to abolish the elevation on account of the
papists who regarded the mass as a sacrifice and a work by us sacrificed
to God, as they still do and have done up until now for over six hundred
years (*WA* 54, 162–63; *LW* 38, 313–14).

This quotation indicates that Luther's principal objections to the Mass
remained unchanged. One may wonder whether both sides would have
been so uncompromising on the question if, in 1537 at Mantua, Luther
had been able to debate his position on behalf of the Protestant princes
and theologians with the Catholic bishops and theologians.

Part I of this study, which this chapter concludes, has presented an
analysis of Luther's works and has shown how he formulated his
theology of the Eucharist, excluding the notion of the Mass as sacrifice.
It has indicated how he further clarified his position by comparison
with the current celebration of the Eucharist and the exercise of the
priesthood, and implemented his convictions in directives to the growing number of Lutheran congregations, and has illustrated how he
maintained his opposition to the Mass as sacrifice in his later confessional writings and in his particular critique of the practice of the
private Mass. Part II will offer a summary and evaluation of Luther's
eucharistic doctrine and will explore the potential of contemporary
research to provide a basis for further doctrinal agreement, particularly
between Lutherans and Roman Catholics.

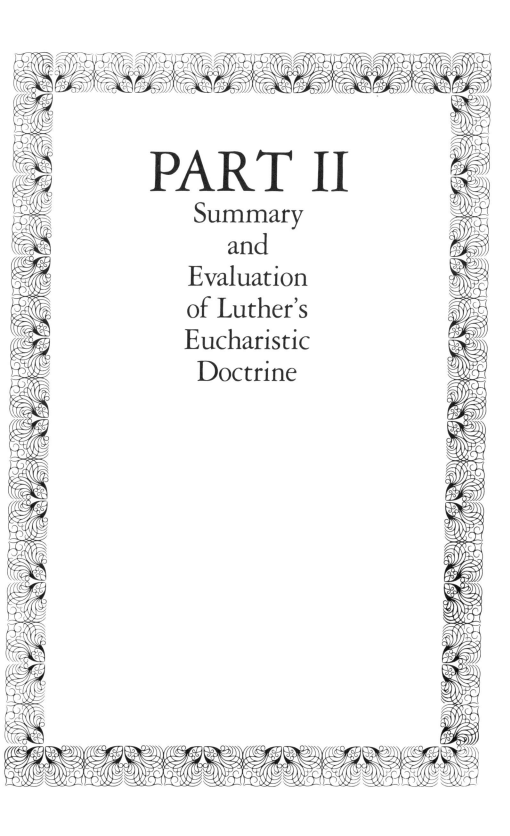

PART II
Summary
and
Evaluation
of Luther's
Eucharistic
Doctrine

CHAPTER IV
THE EUCHARIST AS
TESTAMENT

or Luther, the Eucharist is a testament, a single word that expresses for him the essential meaning of the sacrament. But it is a testament of a special kind: it is a last will, drawn up by Christ at the Last Supper, the night before he died. The terms of the will, its benefits and beneficiaries, were spelled out by Christ in the words he spoke when he instituted the Eucharist on that occasion: "Take, eat; this is my body. . . . Drink of it, all of you; for this is my blood of the [new] covenant, which is poured out for many for the forgiveness of sins" (Matt. 26:26–28). These words contain the promised benefit—the forgiveness of sins; they indicate the beneficiaries—not just the apostles, but the "many," that is, the generations of Christ's followers who would receive the same benefit. And as a pledge and seal of his promise, Christ gives a sign: his body and blood in the form of the bread and wine which he offers to the Twelve.

This brief summary of Luther's doctrine of the Eucharist contains the elements that he considered important and necessary for a sacrament: a promise expressed in the words of Scripture accompanied by a sign instituted by Christ. Any sign, symbol or visible act can be expressive of an invisible reality. But a sign takes on the character of sacrament only when it is combined with the divine word of promise.[1] Since the Eucharist fulfills the qualifications of sign and promise, as well as institution by Christ, it is a sacrament.

---

[1]   Althaus, *The Theology of Martin Luther*, p. 345.

All of this seems clear. But questions arise concerning the components of the sacrament and their relation to one another in Luther's understanding. What is the meaning of the sign, the visible elements of bread and wine as the body and blood of Christ? Does it have any relation to the promise of the forgiveness of sin? Is there any inner connection between the reception of forgiveness and the reception of the sacrament?

In dealing with these questions, Friedrich Graebke many years ago observed a shift of emphasis in the development of Luther's thought. In Luther's earlier works, the body and blood of Christ were the sign of the sacrament, pointing to the word as the vehicle of forgiveness; in later works, the word is the sign, pointing to the body and blood of Christ as the vehicle of forgiveness.[2] As an elaboration on this observation, it is understandable how Luther, while engaged in the "first front" of the Reformation, did stress the Eucharist as the proclamation of the word of forgiveness and the efficacy of our response in faith to such proclamation, against the reliance on the mere performance of the act, the outward reception of the sacrament. Further, while engaged in the "second front" in the controversy concerning the Real Presence, it was important for Luther to give full recognition to the outward elements of the sacrament. In fact, some commentators consider that Luther, at this period of his career, came closest to the Thomist doctrine of sacrament as *signum efficax*.[3]

To say that Luther over-stressed either word of promise or sign would be unfair to him. He was ever aware of the unity of the sacrament.[4] Rather, as has been referred to here, there was a shift in emphasis. But to pursue further the meaning of the sign, the question may be asked: "What connection has the body and blood of Christ with the promise

---

[2] Friedrich Graebke, *Die Konstruction der Abendmahlslehre Luthers in ihrer Entwicklung dargestellt* (Leipzig, 1908), p. 72. Cf. also Schwab, *Entwicklung und Gestalt der Sakramententheologie bei Martin Luther*, pp. 169–84; Quere, "Changes and Constants: Structure in Luther's Understanding of the Real Presence in the 1520's," 45–76.

[3] H. Grass, *Die Abendmahlslehre bei Luther und Calvin* (Gütersloh, 1954), p. 183, cites Luther on the salvific power of water in baptism: "Incredibilis res est, quod in aqua baptismi stecke Gott mit aller seiner Kraft, quod spiritus sanctus sit in eo [sic]" (WA 30[1], 54); he then comments: "Gerade in diesen letzten Formeln kommt Luthers formelle Nähe zum Thomismus am stärksten zum Ausdruck." Cf., also, McDonough, *The Law and the Gospel in Luther*, pp. 124–25.

[4] Cf., for example, *Vom Abendmahl Christi, Bekenntnis*, WA 26, 478–79.

of forgiveness?" Obviously, Christ used this sign to assure us that what was gained for us through his death should belong to us. His body and blood were the very means by which he gained for us the forgiveness of our sins. The importance of the doctrine of the Real Presence here becomes apparent: only when the same body and blood, which were given for us on Calvary, are given to us in the Communion meal is the sign perfectly sure.[5]

But to speak of the body and blood of Christ, and of his death, does this not imply also his self-oblation, his sacrifice? It would seem that the Eucharist, instituted under this sign at the Last Supper, receives its efficacy from the sacrifice of Christ on the following day; hence, this reality is a sacrificial reality.[6] However, although the body and blood of Christ are sacrificial terms, they refer to the body which *has been* given us and the blood which *has been* shed for us in his death.[7] For Luther, then, this sign of the Eucharist as the vehicle of the forgiveness of sins does not primarily concern the act by which such forgiveness was obtained but the effects which flow from that act.[8] Christ is present in the Eucharist under the sign of his body and blood to assure us that the forgiveness obtained on Calvary is extended to us now. The *signum* of the sacrament becomes rather a *sigillum*, a seal of God's promise.[9]

The designation of the Eucharist itself by Luther as Christ's testament or last will will now be considered more closely. The term originates no doubt with the words of institution,[10] but Luther's constant use of the idea to express the meaning of the sacrament, complete with all the requisite elements of a will, prompts the question as to whether he has not couched his explanation of the Eucharist in too legal a framework. This difficulty did not escape the critics of his own day. John Eck, in a manner that characterized his polemical writing, charged that, with this conception of the Eucharist, Luther showed himself as

[5] Regin Prenter, "Luther on Word and Sacrament," in *More About Luther* (Iowa, 1958), p. 115.
[6] Eugene Masure, *The Christian Sacrifice* (London, 1944), p. 239.
[7] Meinhold and Iserloh, *Abendmahl und Opfer*, pp. 64–65.
[8] So Luther is interpreted by Graebke, *Abendmahlslehre Luthers*, pp. 72–73.
[9] This refinement in meaning is made by Regin Prenter, *Spiritus Creator*, trans. John M. Jensen (Philadelphia, 1953), pp. 144–45.
[10] Vajta, *Luther on Worship*, p. 39, n. 43, suggests also that Luther takes the idea of "last will" from a homily of Chrysostom on Heb. 9:13ff. Cf. Luther's own commentary on Hebrews, *WA* 57, 211ff.

poor a jurist as a theologian in having the same people both witnesses
and heirs of the will:

> Here is this unlearned and inexperienced jurist-theologian who, in order
> to destroy the rite of the sacrifice of the Mass of the universal Church,
> reaches such a point of insanity as to make the same persons both wit-
> nesses and heirs, contrary to all legal provisions concerning a will.[11]

More seriously, Eck accused Luther of narrowing the meaning of the
inheritance of Christ by the use of "testament." The inheritance, Luther
says, is the forgiveness of sin; but this is only the means, the necessary
condition, to receiving the positive part of the inheritance, namely,
eternal life. Here, Eck is simply mis-reading Luther who ordinarily
refers to the inheritance as the forgiveness of sin *and* eternal life.[12] In
places where he refers only to the forgiveness of sin, we may easily
presume that he intends eternal life to be understood.[13]

Nevertheless, the explanation of the Eucharist in forensic language
troubles some commentators even today. Regin Prenter questions
whether this interpretation of the Greek word *diatheke* in the words of
institution is a valid philological exegesis.[14] Yngve Brilioth feels that
the testament-idea is especially inadequate when it is applied to the
Last Supper. There is no natural connection between this conception
of the Eucharist and the act of Communion.[15]

Others defend Luther's use of the testament-idea. Vilmos Vajta appeals to Luther's earlier exegetical writing to indicate that he had
in mind a broader notion of testament. Vajta refers with approval to
Luther's commentary on Gal. 3:15 where he identifies testament with

---

[11]   My own translation of a quotation from *Ad invictissimum Poloniae regem Sigismundum, de
sacrificio missae contra Lutheranos* (1525), XLVII r, in Erwin Iserloh's *Die Eucharistie in
der Darstellung des Johannes Eck* (Münster, 1950), p. 169; same quotation in the complete work: Johannes Eck, *De sacrificio missae libri tres* (1526), eds. Erwin Iserloh, Vinzenz Pfnür and Peter Fabisch (Münster, 1982), p. 144.

[12]   Cf., as examples, *Ein Sermon von dem neuen Testament, WA* 6, 358; *ibid.,* pp. 359,
361.

[13]   Iserloh, *Die Eucharistie in der Darstellung des Johannes Eck*, pp. 170–71.

[14]   Prenter, "Luther on Word and Sacrament," p. 113; yet he is clear about Luther's intention: " . . . to indicate that the promise of God made to us in the Eucharist sums
up or consummates . . . all the previous promises made by God in the history of salvation, declaring them all to be fulfilled in the death of Christ" (*ibid*).

[15]   Yngve Brilioth, *Eucharistic Faith and Practice, Evangelical and Catholic*, trans. A. G.
Hebert (London, 1953), p. 102.

the promises of God and contrasts it with the law, and righteousness
which comes by the law. Thus, testament takes on the biblical meaning
of covenant as the sovereign act of God who by his promise accepts us
into fellowship with himself. Next, if God's promises to Abraham
could be called a testament (Gal. 3:17), then they must imply the
incarnation of Christ, for a testament looks to the death of the testator.
The eternal God had to become human and die in order to fulfill the
promise. A direct line of continuity is thereby established between the
words of promise and the words of institution.[16] This argument begins
with an expanded notion of "testament," but ends by casting it in the
legal framework to which objection is made. Further, it must be observed (since Vajta agrees with Luther's exegesis) that Paul in this passage of Galatians plays on the meaning of *diatheke* in a manner just the
reverse of the argument: he begins by using the word in the Hellenistic
sense ("last will and testament") (Gal. 3:15) and shifts to the Septu-
agint sense ("covenant") (Gal. 3:17).[17]

In answer to Brilioth's objection, Vajta asserts that the connection
between the Eucharist as testament and communion is seen when one
considers the role of the heirs. They do not simply admire the inheritance as passive spectators (this attitude would reveal an understanding
of the Eucharist as sacrifice rather than testament). Rather, they receive
it in faith and profit by it.[18] But if they do not receive it, is there still
the testament? Brilioth's further question remains: "Would not the
gift of the testament be equally valid without a physical appropriation
of its sign and seal?"[19]

Carl Wisløff agrees with Vajta's argument on the broader notion of
testament,[20] and contends further that the testament-idea was already in the pre-Reformation tradition. In using it, Luther is simply

---

[16] Vajta, *Luther on Worship*, pp. 40–41. In the second reference to "testament," Gal.
3:18 is indicated in the text, but this must be a mistake or a misprint.
[17] Cf. Joseph A. Fitzmyer, *The Letter to the Galatians. The Jerome Biblical Commentary*,
p. 242.
[18] Vajta, *Luther on Worship*, pp. 42–43.
[19] Brilioth, *Eucharistic Faith and Practice*, p. 102. Vajta concedes this further difficulty
and answers that it stems not from a juridical approach but from the character of
God's activity giving the inheritance a real existence whether or not one believes in
it. But to say this is precisely to remove the discussion from the legal framework of a
will.
[20] Wisløff, *The Gift of Communion*, p. 33.

following in the steps of Gabriel Biel (c. 1420–1495), a theologian
considered to have had a formative influence on the reformer's eucharistic doctrine.[21] Biel *does* conceive of the new testament in the words
of institution according to the image of a last will:

> Concerning the phrase, "of the new and eternal testament," it is to be
> observed that, since a testament is the final distribution of goods estab-
> lished by the death of the testator . . . faith and the covenant of Christ
> are properly called a new testament. For in them Christ promises, ar-
> ranges and distributes his eternal inheritance to his brothers and his
> faithful. This covenant is established by the suffering and death of Christ
> in which his blood was poured out, such shedding of blood being the
> legitimate witness and confirmation of his testament.[22]

On this point, then, Wisløff is correct. But, having shown how Luther
finds support in the tradition, he proceeds to indicate how the reformer
developed his doctrine along very different lines. In its understanding
of *testamentum*, the tradition continued to emphasize the difference between the old and new covenants, the superiority of the new over the
old, reflected in the contrast between the signs of the old covenant and
the sacraments of the new.[23] Luther, on the other hand, tried to maintain a connection between the two covenants, seeing a continuity especially in the promises accompanied by a sign as contrasted with the
prescriptions of works, a continuity in the "sacraments of faith," contrasted with the "sacraments of works." The sign of the Last Supper is
thus in line with the series of promises regarding salvation, from Adam

---

[21] Luther himself later speaks about having read Biel's *Canonis Misse Expositio*: "Gabriel
      scribens librum super canonem missae, qui liber meo iudicio tum optimus fuerat;
      wenn ich darinnen las, da blutte mein hertz. Bibliae autoritas nulla fuit erga Gabriel-
      em. Ich behalte noch die bucher, die mich also gemartert haben" (*WA TR* 3, #3722,
      564). The last two sentences would seem to qualify Luther's recommendation of Biel.
      I would agree with the translation of Theodore G. Tappert in *LW* 54, 264; for an
      unusual translation, with a quite different meaning, cf. Steven Ozment, "Luther and
      the Middle Ages: The Formation of Reformation Thought," in *Transition and Revolu-
      tion*, ed. Robert Kingdon (Minneapolis, 1974), p. 115; repeated in Ozment's *The Age
      of Reform, 1250–1550* (New Haven, Conn., 1980), pp. 231–32.
[22] *Gabrielis Biel Canonis Misse Expositio*, eds. Heiko Oberman and William Courtenay,
      II, Lect. 53N, pp. 324–25; my translation.
[23] Here, Wisløff could have referred again to Biel, *ibid.*, p. 325: "'Novum' dicitur res-
      pectu veteris, quod in institutione huius est terminatum et evacuatum."

to Christ.[24] Luther *did* see an integral relation between the promises of both covenants.[25] But one would think the argument of continuity to be even better served by conceiving the *novum testamentum* not just as a last will and testament, but as another covenant—a "new" and "better" covenant, precisely because it includes the last testament of Christ, sealed by his redeeming death.

Luther's use of the testament-idea to explain the Eucharist will continue to be a point of discussion in the interpretation of his thought. It is clear that such use does not freeze his doctrine in a juridical mould. The image was simply a convenient way (not without precedent in other theologians) to formulate his doctrine. Nevertheless, for some, and especially for contemporary Catholic theologians, his consistent use of it impoverishes the covenant-idea foretold in Jeremiah: "I will make a new covenant with the house of Israel and the house of Judah, not like the covenant I made with their fathers. . . . But this is the covenant which I shall make with the house of Israel after those days, says the Lord: I will put my law within them, and I will write it upon their hearts; and I will be their God, and they shall be my people" (Jer. 31:31–33). Such a covenant is surely one of the forgiveness of sin and the hope of eternal life (Jer. 31:34); but it is also a covenant of union between the covenant parties in the present, a union between God and his people in Christ, the unique mediator of the covenant. And this union ought to be expressed by the Eucharist, the sign of the new covenant—particularly in the act of Communion.

If, for a moment, one assumes with Luther that the Eucharist is conceived as a testament—a promise of forgiveness of sin and eternal life, validated by the death of Christ and given visible and abiding expression in the sign of the testament, the elements of bread and wine as his body and blood—it follows logically that the celebration of the Eucharist, the Mass, cannot be a sacrifice. The Eucharist, as testament, is God's gift to us; it is the inheritance given to the heirs; it is a *beneficium*. The Eucharist, as sacrifice, is just the reverse: it is our gift to God. And since, in this case, the only visible gift of which there can be question is the elements of the sacrament, we presume to offer as gift to God what was intended for us as gift. Such a reversal is a misuse of God's gift; it is a sacrilege. Moreover, since we offer in sac-

---

24   Wisløff, *The Gift of Communion*, pp. 34–35.
25   Cf. *De captivitate Babylonica*, WA 6, 514.

rifice the body and blood of Christ, we in effect presume to crucify the Son of God once again. This action supposes that the sacrifice of Christ offered once for all time is insufficient. It is an insult against God; it is a blasphemy.

However, Luther did not wish to eliminate every trace of the element of sacrifice from the Eucharist. Its celebration could still be considered a sacrifice of praise and thanksgiving, affording us the opportunity of recalling God's grace and mercy and of thanking him through his Son for his gifts. Above all, it is an invitation to those who participate to make an offering of themselves to God, yielding their lives to his will. Yet these elements of sacrifice, Luther is careful to underline, are just associated with the Eucharist in prayers and ceremonies. They must be kept separate from the essential nature of the Eucharist itself, which remains pure gift from God.

The most crucial point in Luther's opposition to the Mass as sacrifice is the basic implication that the Mass is a numerically different sacrifice from that offered once for all by Christ on Calvary. Not only does such an implication conflict with the Mass understood as testament; it underlies Luther's regrets in reflecting on his own experience of having offered Masses, and accounts for the flood of abuses he sees connected with the Mass. In fact, it would be safe to say that it is the common presupposition of Luther's entire critique of the Mass. Yet we find in the tradition before Luther, and in at least some of the Catholic apologists responding to him, an expression of the accepted doctrine, namely, that the sacrifice of Christ and the sacrifice of the Mass are one and the same.

Gabriel Biel makes this point several times in his *Canonis Misse Expositio*. He sees the Mass as the *signum memoriale et representativum* of the supreme sacrifice that Christ offered upon the cross. In one instance, he cites St. Ambrose commenting on Hebrews as support for conceiving the Mass–Calvary relationship in this way, and continues:

> Notice that blessed Ambrose states that it is one sacrifice which Christ offered and which we offer, although it is not offered in the same manner. It was offered by himself in his death; it is offered by us not in his death—for Christ being raised from the dead will never die again (Rom. 6)—but in remembrance of his death. Hence our offering is not a repetition of his offering, but its representation.[26]

---

[26] Biel, *Canonis Misse Expositio*, II, Lect. 53U, p. 332; my translation.

The Mass is related to Calvary as remembrance and representation of Christ's sacrifice. But Biel's use of these terms does not make the Mass a mere memorial of Calvary in the sense of a psychological representation of a past historical event.[27] We must find the meaning of these terms in other statements in which Biel elaborates on the different modes of offering of the one sacrifice. For example:

> Although Christ was offered once in the evident form of his flesh, nevertheless he is offered daily on the altar in the veiled form of bread and wine. Assuredly, he is not offered in a way which involves punishment; for Christ is not daily wounded nor does he suffer and die daily. Rather for two other reasons, namely the consecration and the reception of the Eucharist, is this offering called a sacrifice and oblation. It is such, then, because it is a representation and memorial of that original sacrifice and holy immolation carried out on the cross, and because, as a causal principle, it achieves similar effects.[28]

The Mass is a sacrifice, not because of a physical immolation of Christ, but because of the consecration and communion; the former relates the sacrificial action of the Mass to the immolation on the cross and the latter makes operative effects similar to those that flow from the unique redemptive act. Both relate the Eucharist to the sacrifice of Calvary in a real sense and not just by means of a mental representation. And this relationship establishes the two as different "offerings" of one and the same sacrifice.[29]

Jerome Emser (1478–1527), a Catholic respondent to Luther on the subject of the Mass,[30] distinguishes three ways in which Christ offered himself: *figuraliter*, by eating the paschal lamb with the disciples at the Last Supper, signalling thereby the end of the priesthood and sacrifice of the Jews to make way for a new order; *sacramentaliter*, by blessing the bread and wine at the Supper, instituting the new priesthood and

[27] Cf. Heiko Oberman, *The Harvest of Medieval Theology* (Grand Rapids, Mich., 1967), pp. 271–75, 279–80.
[28] Biel, *Canonis Misse Expositio*, IV, Lect. 85F, p. 101; again, my translation.
[29] *Ibid.*, IV, Lect. 85I, p. 103: "Ecce quantum est sacrificium nostrum, nedum memoriale magni illius unici et perfectissimi sacrificii semel in cruce oblati, sed id ipsum et semper idipsum."
[30] Jerome Emser, *Missae Christianorum contra Lutheranam missandi formulam assertio* (1524), *Corpus Catholicorum* XXVIII.

sacrifice of Christians; and *vere ac realiter*, by dying on the cross, re-
conciling all things to God through his blood (Col. 1:20). Emser agrees
with Luther's main contention that Christ cannot again offer himself
in sacrifice in this last sense. But in the Mass, Christ is offered *sacramentaliter*, in the sense that his body and blood are offered "in mystery,
under the species of bread and wine."[31]

In another work,[32] Emser elaborates somewhat on what he means by
Christ being offered "in mystery." Once more, he is dealing with the
objection that, since Christ cannot die again, there can be no further
sacrifice:

> Where Paul says that Christ will not die nor be sacrificed again, he means
> the circumstances in which, being stripped, he hung in disgrace upon
> the cross and died. Here he did not have in mind the sacrifice of the
> altar in which Christ, after his resurrection, is offered, not in disgrace
> but with great honor and glory, not stripped but clothed and "sub ve-
> lamine" as Paul himself expresses it (Heb. 10:20), under the form of
> bread and wine. For as the Father has given him to us, so may we present
> and offer him again to the Father, from whom he will never more be
> separated.[33]

What is significant here is Emser's reference to the offering of Christ
according to his state after the resurrection. While he does not elaborate
on this dimension, it is clear that he understands a difference between
the way in which Christ was offered on Calvary and the way he is offered
in the Eucharist.

Cardinal Cajetan, whom Luther had met face to face at Augsburg in
1518, dismisses as error the opinion that the sacrifice of the altar
is distinct from that which Christ offered upon the cross. These are one
sacrifice because the same body of Christ and the same blood of Christ
are present on the cross, on the altar and now in heaven.[34] Christ, then,
is both signified and contained in the sacrifice of the altar. But the

---

[31]   *Ibid.*, pp. 17–18.
[32]   *Auff Luthers grewel wider die heiligen Stillmess Antwort* (1525), *Corpus Catholicorum*
       XXVIII.
[33]   *Ibid.*, p. 177; my translation.
[34]   Cardinal Cajetan, *De erroribus contingentibus in eucharistiae sacramento* (1525), *Opuscula
       Omnia*, tom. II, tract. 2, p. 145.

death of Christ is not contained therein, but only signified. It is signified in the words of consecration (". . . which will be shed for you
and for many") and in the separate consecration of the body and blood
of Christ, such sacramental separation signifying the real separation of
his blood from his body in death.[35] Thus, by word and action the
physical immolation of Christ is signified in the sacrifice of the altar.
In this way, as Cajetan states in a later tract,[36] the one sacrifice of Christ
is not repeated but perdures in a special manner of offering:

> To the second argument, on the repetition of offerings, I say that in the
> new covenant the sacrifice or offering is not repeated, but rather there
> continues in the manner of an offering the unique sacrifice offered once
> and for all. In the manner of its continuance a repetition does occur, but
> not in what is offered. Nor does the manner that is repeated constitute
> a sacrifice for itself but for the unbloody commemoration of the offering
> made on the cross.[37]

Gaspar Contarini (1483–1542), himself an advocate of reform in the
Church,[38] likewise attempts to correct Luther's understanding of
the relationship between the Mass and Christ's unique sacrifice.[39] He
insists, with the other apologists, that both constitute the same sacrifice, having the same offering—the body and blood of Christ—and
the same offerer—Christ himself. But he uses other terms in expressing
how both differ in the manner of offering:

> The difference (of the Mass offering) arises not by reason of the sacrifice
> itself—since it is the same sacrifice which is offered—but by reason of
> the manner in which it is offered. For the original sacrifice was offered

---

[35] *Ibid.*, p. 143.

[36] *De missae sacrificio et ritu adversus Lutheranos* (1531), *Opuscula Omnia*, tom. III, tract.
10.

[37] *Ibid.*, p. 287; translation from Wicks, *Cajetan Responds*, p. 198.

[38] Having been made a cardinal in 1535, Contarini was an influential member of the
commission established by Pope Paul III to outline a program of reform for the
Church. In 1537, the commission issued *Consilium de emendanda Ecclesia*, a comprehensive blueprint for reform which laid the blame for most ills of the Church on the
Roman Curia itself. Cf. Robert E. McNally, *The Reform of the Church: Crisis and Criticism in Historical Perspective* (New York, 1963), pp. 120–22; Ozment, *The Age of Reform*, pp. 402–403.

[39] Gaspar Contarini, *Confutatio articulorum seu quaestionum Lutheranorum* (1530), *Corpus
Catholicorum* VII.

> in the form of his humanity in which the Son of God manifested himself,
> but the present sacrifice is offered in the form of bread and wine.[40]

In expressing this difference, Contarini here draws an interesting parallel between the incarnation of Christ and the Eucharist.

A sufficient number of Catholic apologists have been cited here to indicate the uniformity of their teaching regarding the Mass and Calvary. Without revealing any consistent theory of sacrifice, they agree on two points: (1) the sacrifice of the Mass is not to be separated from the sacrifice of the cross as a numerically different sacrifice; (2) the difference between the two sacrifices lies in the manner of offering. The apologists differ in the way in which they conceive and express the manner of offering in both cases. In these variations may be seen a groping towards the formulation settled upon later by the Council of Trent, *oblatio cruenta et incruenta*.[41] These differences of expression left intact the apologists' identification of the Mass with the sacrifice of the cross. On this evidence, Joseph Lortz, allowing for some anthropocentric and moralistic phrasing in the current doctrine of sacrifice, concludes: "Neither the Church nor any individual Catholic theologian had ever asserted that the center of the Mass was a sacrifice made by man."[42]

Why, then, is this assertion a recurring presupposition in Luther's criticism of the Mass? This is a difficult question to answer from across the centuries. The most probable reason is that Luther was constantly concerned to preserve the uniqueness and the all-sufficiency of the sacrifice of the cross. This objective is achieved, and supported by his reading of Scripture, in the conception of the Eucharist as the promise and pledge to us of what was accomplished for us once in that unique sacrifice. Another reason, of some importance, is the fact that Luther's opinions about the Mass were formed more from interpreting the Mass-practice of the day (which, as will be seen in a later chapter, tended to regard the Mass as having an efficacy all its own) than from the tracts of theologians.

---

[40]   *Ibid.*, pp. 17–18; my translation.
[41]   Cf. *Enchiridion Symbolorum*, eds. Henricus Denzinger and Adolphus Schönmetzer (Rome, 1966), #1743, pp. 408–409.
[42]   Lortz, *The Reformation*, I, p. 446.

Misunderstanding of the Catholic teaching about the Mass–Calvary relationship continued in the Lutheran tradition because of a false doctrine attributed to Catholic theologians. According to this doctrine, Christ's sacrifice on the cross expiated only original sin and the sacrifice of the Mass was instituted to expiate personal sin. Were this true, the sacrifice of the Mass would clearly be considered a distinct sacrifice. It could not be said that this doctrine had any formative influence on Luther's criticism of the Mass; his objections were formulated on other grounds before the "error" was brought to public attention by Melanchthon in his *Confessio Augustana* in 1530. There, he refers to the abominable error

> according to which it was taught that our Lord Christ had by his death made satisfaction only for original sin, and had instituted the Mass as a sacrifice for other sins. This transformed the Mass into a sacrifice for the living and the dead, a sacrifice by means of which sin was taken away and God was reconciled. . . . Out of this grew the countless multiplication of Masses, by the performance of which men expected to get everything they needed from God.[43]

The *Confutatio Pontificia*, compiled by Catholic theologians under the leadership of the papal legate Campeggio in answer to the *Confessio*, disclaimed the doctrine entirely:

> Indeed, what is assumed is scarcely understandable, namely, that Christ by his passion had made satisfaction for original sin and had instituted the Mass [to satisfy] for actual sin. This doctrine was never heard of by Catholic [theologians], and the great majority [var. "all"] of those questioned denied very firmly ever having taught it.[44]

Although Luther did not make use of this controverted assertion of Melanchthon after 1530 in his case against the sacrifice of the Mass, he shows that he was familiar with the false doctrine because he used a variation of it in *Von der Winkelmesse* in 1533. In the context, he is discussing not the Mass but the effects of baptism:

---

[43] Translation from the *Book of Concord*, p. 58.
[44] Quoted by B. J. Kidd in *The Later Medieval Doctrine of the Eucharistic Sacrifice* (London, 1958), p. 74; my translation.

> Besides, some of them are now beginning to preach shamelessly the
> blasphemous doctrine that Christ has made satisfaction only for original
> sin and sins prior to baptism; for sins that follow baptism we must
> ourselves make satisfaction (*WA* 38, 226; *LW* 38, 183).

The origin of this peculiar doctrine is unclear.[45] Its authenticity was
denied in the sixteenth century and is likewise denied today.[46] In
view of this, it is indeed curious that such an unsupported opinion has
been retained in the Augsburg Confession of the *Book of Concord*,[47]
perpetuating misunderstanding on an important point of doctrine
which only present-day dialogue between Catholics and Lutherans is
succeeding in dispelling.

---

[45]   The Weimar editor attributes the doctrine, as used by Luther in the preceding quote
       of the text, to a sermon of George Witzel (1501–1573) on October 18, 1533 (*WA*
       38, 226). Melanchthon, in his *Apologia*, attributes it to St. Thomas; cf. the *Book of
       Concord*, p. 260. But Kidd, *The Later Medieval Doctrine*, p. 83, rightly denies such an
       interpretation of a Thomistic text. Cf. also Wicks, *Cajetan Responds*, p. 286, nn. 5 &
       6; Padberg, "Luther und der Canon Missae," 295.
[46]   Reinhold Theisen, *Mass Liturgy and the Council of Trent* (Collegeville, Minn., 1965),
       p. 78: "Melanchthon (in the *Confessio*) cites not a single Catholic theologian who held
       this opinion, and the reason is obvious: there is no evidence that the doctrine was
       ever taught by theologians or even believed by the populace" (parentheses added).
[47]   As above, n. 43.

CHAPTER V
OUR RESPONSE: FAITH

hen Luther describes the Eucharist as a testament, he maintains that our appropriate response to it is faith. Central to the testament is the promise contained in the words of institution. Like the promises of God which preceded it in the Old Testament, the promise of forgiveness of sin and eternal life in the Eucharist is received by us in faith. Faith is exercised in hearing the word of promise with trusting acceptance and in receiving the sacrament itself. In faith we prepare to receive the sacrament; in faith we receive it; through faith we acquire the promised inheritance.

If faith is lacking or absent, the way is open to the abomination of works and to a false, presumptuous trust in them instead of in God's gift. Faith declines when the words of institution are uttered in silence and the inheritance promised therein is not announced to the people. Their faith is not elicited in these circumstances and they come to regard the celebration of the Eucharist as a good work: something they *do* to make themselves pleasing to God or to merit benefits for others.

But, from Luther's perspective, the Mass cannot be a good work. As a testament, the Mass is a benefit received, not given; it is an inheritance received in accordance with a promise made. In receiving and accepting it, one does not *do* anything; one simply receives it in faith, believing that what is contained in the promise becomes one's possession in the appropriation of its sign and pledge, the body and blood of Christ. And faith itself is not a work, but the "lord and life of all works."[1]

---

[1] *De captivitate Babylonica*, WA 6, 520.

At the same time, Luther does not wish to exclude every form of "works" from the Mass. Just as there are "sacrifices" associated with the Mass, so, too, there are "works." These are the prayers we pour out before God when we are gathered together to celebrate the Mass and through which we seek to apply and communicate blessings to one another. Such prayers, however, are distinct from the Mass itself and follow upon the faith which it, as testament, has aroused:

> Now these are not the mass, but works of the mass—if the prayers of heart and lips may be called works—for they flow from the faith that is kindled or increased in the sacrament. For the mass, or the promise of God, is not fulfilled by praying but only by believing. However, as believers we pray and perform every good work (WA 6, 522; LW 36, 50).

As in the case of the "sacrifices" of the Mass, Luther realizes that this distinction is commonly overlooked and soon the Mass itself is regarded as a work. The priest, in offering the Mass, and the people, in attending it, consider that they are performing a good work for all those whom they intend to benefit.

When the Mass itself is regarded as a good work, Luther detects in this attitude a basic premise that runs counter to the way of salvation: the principle of works-righteousness whereby we presume to save ourselves. Such a principle is totally unacceptable. One of the chief articles of faith[2] is that Christ accomplished the work of our salvation when he died on the cross for our sins and was raised for our justification. This work of salvation is completed and we lay hold of its benefits by faith alone. Specifically, in the Eucharist, we accept in faith the forgiveness of sin and eternal life, our inheritance as from a testament. But when we regard the Eucharist as a good work, we spurn this gift and scorn the completed work of salvation. We come before God, not to receive his grace in faith but to perform a good work in which we put our trust. This attitude is not piety but impiety; it is not worship but idolatry.[3] The principle of works-righteousness confronts the principle of justification by faith alone.[4]

---

[2]   Stated by Luther in *Die Schmalkaldischen Artikel, WA* 50, 198–99.
[3]   Vajta, *Luther on Worship*, p. 58.
[4]   Wisløff, *The Gift of Communion*, pp. 54–55.

The foregoing argument of Luther would have considerable validity were it not for the fundamental flaw which neglects to understand that the Mass is primarily the work of Christ. Just as the Mass as sacrifice cannot be separated from the sacrifice of Christ, so the Mass as a good work cannot be separated from the work of Christ. Was this relationship between the two so understood in Luther's day? While the Mass-practice of the time often betrayed it, some theologians did maintain a proper understanding. Gabriel Biel, for example, expressed it quite clearly, attributing the efficacy of any meritorious work to the unique and perfect sacrifice of Christ:

> In this [eucharistic] sacrifice, there is a memorial of and a reliance upon that unique and most perfect sacrifice [of Christ], through the efficacy of which the heavens are opened and grace is given; through which alone all our works can be meritorious, all sins forgiven and heavenly glory, lost by our sins, restored. . . . No work, after the original fall, could ever be pleasing and acceptable to God the Father, except in the power of this evening sacrifice, offered until the end of the world (Col. 1:19–20).[5]

As the efficacy of any meritorious work stems from the sacrifice of Christ, so the continued offering of this sacrifice, as a "work," is one with the original work of Christ.

Cardinal Cajetan, in responding to Luther, affirmed that the sacrifice of Christ on Calvary perdures in the sacrifice of the Mass. Going one step further, he also affirmed that the all-sufficiency of Christ's work perdures in the Eucharist:

> To the third argument, concerning what is offered, we respond that Christ's abundant and all-sufficient shedding of his own blood once and for all on the cross fits quite well with the continuation of that unique and all-sufficient shedding of blood on the cross in the Eucharist in the manner of an offering.[6]

The celebration of the Eucharist is, then, primarily the work of Christ. It is the work of the celebrant and those who participate only in the

---

5 Biel, *Canonis Misse Expositio*, II, Lect. 57D, pp. 395–96; my translation.
6 Cajetan, *De missae sacrificio, Opuscula Omnia*, tom. III, tract. 10, p. 287; translation from Wicks, *Cajetan Responds*, p. 199.

sense that Christ has directed that they share with him the renewed offering of himself to the Father.[7]

Luther's strong emphasis on faith as our response to the Eucharist implied a corollary that involved additional differences from the Catholic tradition. Faith is a personal response of the individual. Therefore, when a person accepts with faith the promise contained in the Eucharist, he does so for himself alone; he cannot accept, apply or communicate the benefit to another. Catholic tradition, on the other hand, taught (and continues to teach) that by offering the Mass the faithful benefit not only themselves but others, both living and dead. Luther, in eliminating the Mass as sacrifice, eliminated its application to the living and the dead.

He arrived at a firm position on this question somewhat gradually. In 1520, he simply registers his doubt as to whether requiem Masses for the souls in purgatory can continue without abuse, since they are regarded as good works by which to recompense God. The faithful may nevertheless pray for the souls of the departed in a spirit of faith, because faith that relies on the promise of Christ never fails.[8] In 1525, he takes a strong stand against applying the Mass to the living: one prayer of the Canon recommends for benefit those whose faith and devotion are known to God; but if they already have faith, they are redeemed and have no need of the benefits of the Mass.[9] In 1528, he regards it as no sin to pray for the dead, that God may be gracious and merciful to them; but this is all that may be done. Requiem Masses and yearly remembrances in Masses are useless and merely the devil's annual fair.[10] In this development, Luther is consistent with his theology of the Eucharist. We may pray for the dead because prayers are the acceptable "works" associated with the Mass but separate from it. The Mass itself, as testament, rests on the faith of each individual and can benefit that person alone.

Luther's position on the effects of the Mass is understandable when one realizes that for him the Eucharist was *sacramentum* only. Catholic tradition had been accustomed to distinguishing the Eucharist as *sacramentum* and as *sacrificium* and, on the basis of this distinction (re-

7   Cf. Meinhold and Iserloh, *Abendmahl und Opfer*, p. 86.
8   *Ein Sermon von dem neuen Testament*, WA 6, 371–72.
9   *Vom Greuel der Stillmesse*, WA 18, 26.
10 *Vom Abendmahl Christi, Bekenntnis*, WA 26, 508.

garding the Mass as *sacrificium*), teaching its efficacy for others, both the living and the dead. Thomas Aquinas expressed this distinction succinctly as follows:

> This sacrament is both a sacrifice and a sacrament; it has the nature of a sacrifice inasmuch as it is offered up; and it has the nature of a sacrament inasmuch as it is received. And therefore it has the effect of a sacrament in the recipient, and the effect of a sacrifice in the offerer, or in them for whom it is offered.[11]

Aquinas would therefore agree with Luther that the Eucharist as sacrament benefits only the one who receives it, and he would undoubtedly agree further that the amount of benefit would be dependent upon the dispositions of the recipient—including personal faith. Yet, in addition, the Eucharist has, for Aquinas, the dimension of sacrifice, and here the whole salvific work of Christ is virtually available to us. Gabriel Biel was also very much aware of this dimension of the Eucharist and describes it in the following manner, after making a distinction similar to that of Aquinas:

> The sacrament is called both a sacrifice and a eucharist: a "sacrifice" because of the remission of sins; a "eucharist" because of the infusion of grace. The former implies the element of merit, not so much from the celebrant as from what is celebrated, for it has the effect of expiating sin, not just from the devotion of the celebrant but much more from the offering itself, that is, from Christ offered anew in memory of his blessed passion, the effect of which is not diminished by any lack of disposition of the priest, observing the rite and intention of the Church. For although it is usual for all the sacraments of the new covenant to have their effect *ex opere operato*, even more so is it appropriate for this sacrament as sacrifice which truly and really contains Christ, both as priest and sacrifice, presenting himself to the Father and offering himself on our behalf as a holocaust, as the apostle states in *Hebrews*.[12]

Here Biel strongly emphasizes the *opus operatum* aspect of the Eucharist as sacrifice, but not to the exclusion of the subjective dispositions of the priest celebrating. Aquinas had maintained a better balance:

---

[11] Thomas Aquinas, *Summa Theologica*, III, q. 79, a. 5; translation by the Fathers of the English Dominican Province, *Summa Theologica*, Vol. II (New York, 1947), p. 2483.
[12] Biel, *Canonis Misse Expositio*, II, Lect. 57D, p. 396; my translation.

In so far as it [the Eucharist] is a sacrifice, it has a satisfactory power. Yet in satisfaction, the affection of the offerer is weighed rather than the quantity of the offering. . . . Therefore, although this offering suffices of its own quantity to satisfy for all punishment, yet it becomes satisfactory for them for whom it is offered, or even for the offerers, according to the measure of their devotion, and not for the whole punishment.[13]

Attention to the devotion of those offering the Mass and of those for whom it is offered safeguards the application of the Mass as sacrifice from being an exercise of magic or superstition. As a doctrine, the application of the Mass asserts simply that the saving grace of Christ's atoning work is made available to the members of his body, living and dead, through the mediation of Christ himself primarily, together with the prayerful intercession of other members, likewise united to him in faith and devotion.[14]

This doctrine concerning the efficacy of the Mass as sacrifice was reaffirmed by the Council of Trent,[15] and has remained the constant teaching of the Catholic tradition. Some aspects receive greater attention at times than others. In current theology, interest has been shown in clarifying the basis for the "fruits" of the Mass—the traditional term for the benefits, for oneself and others, derived from offering the Mass. It is not surprising that theological reflection here has stressed the importance of Christ's original salvific act, as well as the union in faith and love among his people which is effected by that act. Karl Rahner has articulated the foundation of the discussion as follows:

Union by grace in faith and love with Christ's sacrifice is the *one* effect of the sacrifice itself, the essentially single fruit of the sacrifice issuing from the sacrifice itself. Only on this basis is it possible to conceive a

---

[13] Aquinas, *Summa Theologica*, III, q. 79, a. 5; translation by the Fathers of the English Dominican Province, *op. cit.*, p. 2483. Cajetan concurs in affirming the finite value of the Mass as sacrifice: "Si autem sumatur hoc sacrificium ut applicatum isti vel illi, sic effectus eius est finitus iuxta quantitatem devotionis offerentium, vel eorum, pro quibus offertur" (*De missae celebratione* [1509–1510], *Opuscula Omnia*, tom. II, tract. 3, p. 147).

[14] Biel, in another place, adequately summarizes this doctrine: "Quidquid Christus salvator noster meruit se offerens in cruce pro omnibus generaliter, tam in remotione mali, quam in collatione boni viatoribus, purgandis, beatis, hoc sacrificio applicatur particulariter singulis" (*Canonis Misse Expositio*, IV, Lect. 85L, p. 106).

[15] Denzinger and Schönmetzer, *Enchiridion Symbolorum*, #1743, pp. 408–409.

division of the efficacy of the sacrifice into various fruits of the Mass among all those taking part, the celebrant, those present and cooperating in offering the sacrifice, and the faithful who share in it through the intention. For God's love in Christ for man is differentiated in its effects in each case according to the particular needs of the person who offers the Mass or causes it to be offered.[16]

With this perspective, Rahner turns his attention to Masses for the dead, an application that presents special problems. As a general postulate, Masses celebrated for the dead are intercessory: they depend on God's mercy alone and the degree to which that mercy permits the fruits of the Mass to benefit them. On the subjective side, the measure of the benefit received from a Mass depends not upon the disposition of the faithful departed at Mass during life but the disposition of the living who are offering Mass.[17] This condition assumes a close bond between the living and those who have passed to a future life:

> In actual fact the conception of grace which is attested by the Masses for the dead in the Roman liturgy implies awareness of our communion with those who have died in Christ, and the belief that we are able to be close and helpful to them by celebrating Mass *for* the dead. By that Mass, they are drawn afresh into communion with Christ who overcame death in death and whose communion with the dead leads to resurrection; that is the communion which for early Christians was *pax* and *communio* absolutely.[18]

It is this close association of the living with the dead which enables the former to assist the latter through the mediation of the sacrificial action of Christ, leading them through death to resurrection. In eliminating the Mass as sacrifice, Luther logically eliminated this fraternal assistance based upon the communion of saints. He did indeed speak in eloquent terms of the fellowship of the saints,[19] but it was a fellowship resulting from the reception of the Eucharist as sacrament with personal faith. With this fellowship Catholic tradition would concur;

---

[16] Karl Rahner and Angelus Häussling, *The Celebration of the Eucharist*, trans. W. J. O'Hara (New York, 1968), p. 78.

[17] *Ibid.*, p. 81.

[18] *Ibid.*, p. 82.

[19] Particularly in his early *Ein Sermon von dem hochwürdigen Sakrament*, WA 2, 743.

but it would also look to another basis of fellowship: sharing with all the saints, living and dead, the on-going redemptive act of Christ.

Chapters IV and V of this study have drawn together the principal reasons for Luther's opposition to the Mass as a sacrifice and as a good work. And it is important to note that his reasons vary somewhat in treating these two aspects of the Eucharist. Vilmos Vajta and Carl Wisløff, two Lutheran interpreters, do not agree on the meaning Luther gave to the terms "sacrifice" and "work." Vajta considers them used interchangeably by Luther, thus resulting in the same basic objection to the Mass;[20] Wisløff detects different nuances of meaning in the usage of the terms, resulting in a two-pronged attack on the Mass.[21] This difference of interpretation is of considerable importance in exposing and evaluating Luther's criticism of the Mass.

From the treatment, in these last two chapters, of the material unearthed in the analyses of earlier chapters, it is evident that I agree with Wisløff's interpretation.[22] This chapter will conclude by bringing together the arguments in support of his position and supplementing them with my own refinements, based upon the writings of Luther.

The following arguments point to some difference of meaning of the terms "sacrifice" and "work" as used by Luther with reference to the Mass:

(1) In two important tracts written during the period when Luther was formulating his new theology of the Eucharist, *Ein Sermon von dem neuen Testament* (1520) and *De captivitate Babylonica* (1520), he treats the Mass as sacrifice and as work—at least in some sections—as different abuses.[23] Supporting this evidence is the fact that some of Luther's critics read his remarks as separate charges.[24]

---

[20]   Vajta, *Luther on Worship*, pp. 54–58.

[21]   Wisløff, *The Gift of Communion*, pp. 41, 70–71.

[22]   This position is supported also by Wolfgang Schwab, *Entwicklung und Gestalt der Sakramententheologie bei Martin Luther*, pp. 195–96, and is illustrated by his separate treatment of Luther's critique of the Mass as a good work (pp. 194–205) and as a sacrifice (pp. 205–26).

[23]   *Ein Sermon von dem neuen Testament*, WA 6, 364 (work), 365 (sacrifice); *De captivitate Babylonica*, WA 6, 513–23 (work) and 523–26 (sacrifice).

[24]   Wisløff, *The Gift of Communion*, p. 197, n. 8, cites the example of the *Assertio Septem Sacramentorum* of Henry VIII, which defends the Mass first as *sacrificium* and then as *opus*.

(2) To consider the Mass as sacrifice and as work yields different results in Luther's view. Considered as a sacrifice, the Mass results in sacrilege: it misuses the gift of God to us by offering it to God as our gift.[25] Considered as a work, it results in the doctrine of works-righteousness: works take the place of faith.[26]

(3) The Mass as sacrifice misuses the very elements of the sacrament, the body and blood of Christ, regarding them as the victim offered once again in sacrifice.[27] The Mass as work stands in opposition to the doctrine of justification by faith alone; we cannot earn our own salvation.[28] Extending this parallel, one could say that the Mass as sacrifice involves the external aspect of the Eucharist, the outward sign and seal of the promise, while the Mass as work involves the internal aspect, the promise itself in the words of institution, the sum and substance of the gospel.

These arguments indicate a significant variation of meaning in Luther's use of the terms "sacrifice" and "work." At the same time, however, it must be readily acknowledged that Luther frequently uses both terms together. Such instances express his general and complete opposition to the Mass: as *sacrificium* and as *opus*, the Mass is opposed to his understanding of the Eucharist as testament. The former suggests a human-to-God movement in the way of salvation; the latter admits only a God-to-human movement.[29]

---

[25] *Ibid.*, p. 70.
[26] *Ibid.*, pp. 54–55.
[27] *Ibid.*, pp. 70–71.
[28] *Ibid.*, pp. 54–55.
[29] Cf. *De captivitate Babylonica*, WA 6, 526.

CHAPTER VI
THE PRIESTHOOD

istorically, sacrifice and priesthood go together. In the Old Testament, where there was a sacrifice, there was a priest who offered the sacrifice; without a priest there could be no sacrifice. Since Luther was opposed to the dimension of sacrifice in the Eucharist, it is understandable that he would question the priestly function attributed to the minister of the sacrament. And in reverse order of consideration, his conclusion that there is no visible priesthood in the New Testament was one of his strongest arguments against the Mass as sacrifice. Because of this interconnection between priesthood and sacrifice, it is appropriate at this stage to summarize Luther's teaching on priesthood and to enquire in what way it differed from the Catholic tradition on the subject.

Luther admits that only two kinds of priesthood have been instituted by God. One was the outward priesthood of the Old Testament, the Levitical priesthood in which Aaron was high priest. The other is the spiritual priesthood of the New Testament which replaced the Levitical priesthood. Its high priest is Christ, who offered the unique sacrifice when he suffered death upon the cross to obtain for us forgiveness of sin and eternal life. His sacrifice is the only outward and visible sacrifice of the New Testament and he the only priest, the only mediator between God and his people. All Christians who believe in Christ share in this priesthood of Christ and their sharing constitutes a spiritual priesthood: "Come to him, to that living stone, rejected by men but in God's sight chosen and precious; and like living stones be yourselves built into a spiritual house, to be a holy priesthood, to offer spiritual

sacrifices acceptable to God through Jesus Christ" (I Pet. 2:4–5). Since
the basis of this priesthood is faith, all Christians are equally priests;
Scripture gives no support for a clerical order of priests deriving their
power to offer sacrifice from consecration by a bishop.

The consecration that makes all Christians priests is received in baptism. With this sacrament, priests are not made but born, not ordained but created. By the washing of regeneration, they are born not
of the flesh, but of the Spirit. By virtue of their baptism, they are able
to offer acceptable "sacrifices" to God—the sacrifice of praise and
thanksgiving and, above all, the sacrifice of themselves according to
Rom. 12:1: "Present your bodies as a living sacrifice, holy and acceptable to God, which is your spiritual worship." But their function
as priests concerns not only God but their neighbour. It includes also
the task of preaching the word to others. Every Christian has the right
and duty to teach, instruct and admonish his neighbour with the word
of God at every opportunity and whenever necessary.[1] This aspect of
the priesthood of all Christians safeguards Luther's doctrine from being
pure individualism. It does not mean that every Christian is his own
priest, needing no mediator between God and himself; rather, it means
that every Christian is a priest to every other Christian and a mediator
between him and God.[2] This serving of one's neighbour flows from the
reception of the Eucharist and, as an aspect of the priesthood (it must
be stressed again), is separate from the celebration of the Eucharist.

But what of the pastors who preach the word and administer the
sacraments? In what way do they differ from other Christians when
they perform these functions? Pastors are said to hold an office in the
Church. For the sake of order and harmony, certain individual Christians are singled out because of their qualifications (since not everyone
is competent to preach the word) to exercise this office of ministry.
They perform the duties of their office in the spiritual kingdom in
much the same way as their counterparts in the temporal kingdom.[3]

---

[1] Wisløff, *The Gift of Communion*, p. 77.

[2] Jaroslav Pelikan, *Luther the Expositor: Introduction to the Reformer's Exegetical Writings* (St.
     Louis, 1959), pp. 245–46. Also, on the same point, Althaus, *The Theology of Martin
     Luther*, p. 314: "The priesthood means: We stand before God, pray for others, in-
     tercede with and sacrifice ourselves to God and proclaim the word to one another."

[3] Vajta, *Luther on Worship*, pp. 110–11. Cf., also, Hellmut Lieberg, *Amt und Ordination
     bei Luther und Melanchthon* (Göttingen, 1962), pp. 74–76.

Luther's favourite example is that of the mayor of a city. He does not become a citizen in being elected mayor; rather, he is elected mayor because he is a citizen and carries out the administrative duties entrusted to him in the service of the citizenry. Similarly, pastors do not become priests in assuming the office of ministry; they became priests when they were baptized. They carry out the spiritual duties of this office in the service of their fellow Christians and when they are no longer able to preach and serve, or no longer wish to do so, they once more become part of the common multitude of Christians.[4]

Traditionally, after a priest was ordained by a bishop, he was also designated to the office of pastor by a bishop. Luther held that, failing this designation, the congregation itself could select a candidate for the office. His teaching on this point is clearly expressed in his advice to the Bohemian brethren of Prague.[5] In such a situation, the ceremony of ordination signifies the public acknowledgement of the candidate's call to the *Pfarrampt* and his acceptance of the duties of this office.

Here, the question is raised among interpreters as to whether Luther's understanding of the ministry should be called institutional or sociological. Is the office of ministry a divine institution or a human appointment?[6] Interpretations vary in the resolution of this question in the Lutheran tradition, principally because evidence for one side or the other can be given from Luther's writings.[7] The question usually leads to a discussion of the call of the candidate to the office. Here

---

[4] *Der CX Psalm, WA* 41, 208–10. Beyond this functional role, some commentators say that Luther favoured some form of ordination, especially for the celebration of the Eucharist. Cf. Peter Manns, "Amt und Eucharistie in der Theologie Martin Luthers," in Peter Bläser, *Amt und Eucharistie* (Paderborn, 1973), 83–84.

[5] *De instituendis ministris Ecclesiae, WA* 12, 191. Gert Haendler, in *Luther on Ministerial Office and Congregational Function*, trans. Ruth C. Gritch, ed. Eric W. Gritch (Philadelphia, 1981), traces this "congregational" emphasis of Luther's concept of ministry, arguing a consistency in his position even in cases where Luther appeals to the authority of the prince, bishop or city council to appoint a pastor. Cf. especially pp. 68–76.

[6] Vajta, *Luther on Worship*, p. 113.

[7] Brian Gerrish, in "Priesthood and Ministry in the Theology of Luther," *Church History* XXXIV (December 1965), 404–22, reviews the evidence for both sides of this question presented in secondary material since the nineteenth century, and shows how each appeals to Luther's writings for support. As his own solution, Gerrish favours a healthy tension between the view that ministry originates from delegation by the community and the view that it is of divine institution. So also Lieberg, *Amt und Ordination*, pp. 235–39.

again, there is ambiguity. Does the call originate ultimately with the congregation or does it come from God? Wisløff speaks about a "call to public service" having almost the same meaning as "office."[8] Vajta states clearly that the call comes from God, and he sees the resolution of the question in Luther's idea of cooperation: although the call comes from God, it comes also through the people, whether congregation or bishop, who are only instruments in the hand of God.[9] According to this view, the question of the institutional or sociological concepts of ministry was foreign to Luther and represents inconsistencies discovered by later minds. Vajta's solution, while plausible, raises further questions. The divine call would constitute a personal grace to the candidate. Is this grace externalized and (given its repetition in numerous cases) institutionalized in the conferral of office, in the rite of ordination? If so, how is this consistent with Luther's teaching that the only requisite for exercising the ministry of priesthood (apart from accepting the office) is the sacrament of baptism?

The foregoing account of Luther's doctrine of the priesthood of Christ and the priesthood of all believers demonstrates that it represents a departure in some significant aspects from the traditional doctrine of the priesthood. Yet, there are some points of agreement: that there is only one priesthood of the New Testament; that Christ is the eternal high priest of this priesthood; and that all Christians somehow share his priesthood and constitute "a chosen race, a royal priesthood, a holy nation" (I Pet. 2:9). The points of difference mainly concern how the priesthood of Christ is shared with his people, how it is exercised in the Church, and especially how in this exercise a special role is assigned to consecrated priests acting as *vicarii Christi*.

Christ is the eternal high priest of the New Testament. For Luther, he has this title because of the unique sacrifice of the cross which he offered once for all. In Catholic tradition, since the sacrifice of the

---

8   Wisløff, *The Gift of Communion*, p. 77: "The special thing about the one who occupies an office in the church is not that he is a priest, because all Christians are priests, but rather that he has received a call to public service with those functions which belong to all Christians."

9   Vajta, *Luther on Worship*, p. 115. Luther's notion of vocation, as expressed here by Vajta, has some similarity to the "Internal Theory" of vocation, favoured by Catholic tradition: a vocation is a call from God in the form of a special grace, which is confirmed by legitimate ecclesiastical authority. Cf. C. A. Schleck, *New Catholic Encyclopedia* XIV, s.v. "Vocation, Religious and Clerical," p. 735.

Eucharist is virtually the same as the sacrifice of Christ on the cross—
virtually the same redemptive work of Christ—he has this title by
reason of a past yet continuing action. So did the primitive Church
conceive the Eucharist. It was seen essentially as an action, and the
Church in performing that action was simply Christ's body performing
what he willed. Therefore the eucharistic action was necessarily his
action of sacrifice and what was offered must be what he offered. The
Eucharist as sacrament results from the Eucharist as sacrifice; the presence of the body and blood of Christ results from the sacrificial action
of Christ.[10] This same conception of the Eucharist as the action of Christ
is found in the writings of the pre-Nicene Fathers of the Church.[11]
Without losing sight of the basic assumption that the action in the
Eucharist is that of Christ, later tradition also emphasized that Christ
committed this action to his Church with the injunction: "Do this in
remembrance of me" (Lk. 22:19). The offering of Christ became also
the offering of his Church. This was the predominant character of the
eucharistic sacrifice on the eve of the Reformation:

> La messe apparaît de plus en plus nettement, à la veille de la Réforme,
> comme l'oblation faite par l'Eglise, sur l'ordre et dans la puissance du
> Christ, de la victime jadis immolée au Calvaire, offerte de nouveau sur
> l'autel en union avec tous les membres du corps mystique, en vue de
> commémorer en la représentant l'unique immolation réelle rédemptrice
> de la croix, pour nous en appliquer les fruits, nous rendre ainsi Dieu
> propice et nous unir à Lui.[12]

Since the offering of Christ is shared with his Church and is a present
offering, Catholic tradition recognized an order of priests who, by
virtue of a divine call mediated through the Church by sacramental

---

[10] Gregory Dix, *The Shape of the Liturgy* (London, 1970[10]), p. 246. Hence arises the
anomaly for the Catholic tradition of the position of some Reformers who, as Luther,
affirmed and defended the Real Presence of Christ in the Eucharist, yet denied its
sacrificial dimension. The implications of this anomaly are explored by Pratzner,
Messe und Kreuzesopfer, especially pp. 83–118. Cf., also, Meyer, *Luther und die Messe*,
pp. 165–66.

[11] Dix, *ibid.*, p. 253: "I think I can state as a fact that . . . there is no pre-Nicene author Eastern or Western whose eucharistic doctrine is at all fully stated, who does not
regard the offering and consecration of the eucharist as the present action of our Lord
Himself, the Second Person of the Trinity."

[12] A. Gaudel, "L'Idée catholique de la Messe à la Veille de la Réforme," *Dictionnaire de
Théologie Catholique* X, 1, cols. 1081–82.

consecration, make this offering in Christ's name and as representatives of his body, the Church. Priests and laity, therefore, do not participate in the offering of the Church in the same way. Theologians have expressed their respective functions in different ways. Biel, for example, whose treatise on the Mass was familiar to Luther, explained their roles in these terms:

> There are two ways of offering: one, immediately and personally, the other mediately and principally. The first is the way of the priest who consecrates and consumes the sacrament, who, although with divine authority, celebrates in person in such a way that no one else concurs with him in this way of offering. To offer mediately and principally is the way of the church militant, in whose name the priest offers and for whom he is the minister in offering. For the sacrifice offered is that of the whole church, indicated by the fact that the priest does not say, "I pray," but "we pray," in the name of the church.[13]

In support of this special role exercised by priests in offering the Eucharist, Biel argues elsewhere[14] that the injunction "facite," following the words of institution, was spoken only to the apostles. As this injunction has the force of "conficite," Christ thereby committed to them, and to those who would succeed them, the power of consecration. But in doing so, Christ did not relinquish his unique role as eternal high priest:

> Our priests are vicars of the high priest, and in the words they pronounce the uncreated Word makes the offering. . . . By this offering, the human priest performs his ministry. Yet the invisible and chief priest is Christ who changes the bread and wine into the substance of his body and blood.[15]

Here, the visible and the invisible priesthood work in concert to effect one and the same sacrificial action. Luther denied any visible priesthood in the New Testament and maintained that any further offering by Christ of himself was unnecessary. Only the spiritual sacrifices of all Christians remain.

---

[13]   Biel, *Canonis Misse Expositio*, I, Lect. 26H, p. 245; my translation.
[14]   *Ibid.*, II, Lect 53X, p. 333.
[15]   *Ibid.*, IV, Lect. 85H, p. 103; my translation.

In the controversial literature that accompanied Luther's writing, theologians reaffirmed the doctrinal points concerning the priesthood which he had challenged. John Fisher, Bishop of Rochester (1469–1535), in his *Sacri Sacerdotii Defensio contra Lutherum* (1525), while conceding that all Christians are priests in some sense, argues for a ministerial priesthood:

> We concede that in a certain sense it is true that every Christian can truly be said to be a priest. Nevertheless, besides this priesthood which is common to each . . . there must be a special priesthood exercised by those who are legitimately called, ordained and missioned by the rulers of the Church, and who are priests not just in their own right but for the people to whom they minister as a proper vocation.[16]

Cardinal Cajetan stresses the primacy of the priesthood of Christ in describing the role of priestly ministers:

> . . . in the new covenant there is one priest, Christ. He is priest at our altar, since the ministers do not consecrate the body and blood of Christ in their own persons but in the person of Christ, as the words of consecration clearly show. They offer, acting in Christ's place. The priest does not say, "This is the body of Christ," but, "This is my body." In Christ's person he makes present the body of Christ under the form of bread, following the precept of Christ, "Do this."[17]

These quotations from Fisher and Cajetan underline two principal points of the traditional teaching on the priesthood: first, that, in addition to the priesthood of all Christians (an aspect little emphasized at this time), there is a ministerial priesthood wherein priests offer the sacrifice of the New Testament as *praesides ecclesiae*; secondly, that these priests perform this function *in persona Christi*, acting vicariously for Christ himself who remains the unique priest of this sacrifice and the sole mediator of salvation to God's people. This latter point was little appreciated by Luther, even in the earlier days of his own ministry. His

---

[16] John Fisher, *Sacri Sacerdotii Defensio contra Lutherum, Corpus Catholicorum* IX, p. 52; my translation.
[17] Cajetan, *De missae sacrificio, Opuscula Omnia*, tom. III, tract. 10, p. 287; translation from Wicks, *Cajetan Responds*, p. 198.

first Mass in 1507 was a traumatic experience. So great was his fear at
the thought of addressing the Father directly, that only the presence
of the prior prevented him from fleeing the altar. Later, in his *Table
Talk*, he recalls and describes the anguish of that situation:

> Later when I stood there during the mass and began the canon, I was so
> frightened that I would have fled if I hadn't been admonished by the
> prior. For when I read the words, "Thee, therefore, most merciful Father,"
> etc. and thought I had to speak to God without a Mediator, I felt like
> fleeing from the world like Judas. Who can bear the majesty of God
> without Christ as Mediator?[18]

The answer to Luther's question is contained in the very words of the
Canon that immediately follow those which horrified him: "Therefore,
most merciful Father, we humbly beg and entreat you through Jesus
Christ your Son, our Lord . . . ." The words "through Jesus Christ,"
which begin and end the Roman Canon, make it clear that Christ is
the mediator of the eucharistic action.[19] Without this perspective of
Christ as chief priest and mediator in celebrating the Eucharist, the
main criticisms of Luther concerning the Mass fall logically into place:
the Mass is a good work of the priest in which he presumes to offer
Christ in sacrifice once again to the Father, thereby setting up himself
as mediator of God's grace to us—an awesome task and, if one were to
weigh its implications, one calculated to engender fear and dread. With
this supposed context, it is not just exaggeration when Luther refers
to the pope as the anti-Christ, the one who, by claiming from Peter
the power to delegate and consecrate priests to offer the sacrifice of the
Mass in this manner, has obliterated the priesthood of Christ and established his own in its place.[20]

The offering of the *ecclesia militans*, the offering of priestly ministers
as *praesides ecclesiae*, the self-offering of Christ, the eternal priest—
these are the main elements that constitute the sacrifice of the Eucharist
as the offering of the Church. These same elements continued to be
emphasized in Catholic tradition from the time of the Reformation into
the present century, when the full blossoming of the doctrine of the

---

[18]   *WA TR* 3, 410–11; *LW* 54, 234.
[19]   Cf., also, Padberg, "Luther und der Canon Missae," 299–300.
[20]   *Vom Missbrauch der Messe, WA* 8, 486.

Mystical Body offered a congenial framework for explaining the Eucharist as the offering of the Church and for maintaining the elements in proper balance. For example,

> Christ the head communicates to the body that power which He put forth at that very moment when He gave Himself over to death for the life of the world. Hence it is that we offer the Body of Christ which died and was taken up into the glory of God. Therefore, just as His sacerdotal power by which He was ordained, in the things that pertain to God, to offer gifts, is the principal cause of our power, so, too, on the exercise of that same power, which He put forth only once, depends our sacerdotal activity in every Mass. The offering of Christ is the principal and universal cause in its own order; our offering is the subordinate and particular cause.[21]

Because of sensitivity to the developments of christology, more contemporary expressions of the Eucharist as the offering of the Church likewise stress the role of Christ as priest, but do so in terms that recall emphases of the previous tradition. Thus, we find the celebration of the Eucharist explained primarily as the personal sacrificial action of Christ—a characterization which, as we have seen above, was appreciated by the primitive Church:

> In the celebration of the Eucharist, it is Christ's own sacrificial act which is offered to God by Christ, who associates His Church with Himself in this perfect act of worship. That sacrificial act took place in history, it is true, and is not something which can be renewed in such a way that it is present here and now. But as a personal action of the Son of God, that action does possess a timeless dimension which is real in the timeless existence of the Son. It is with this reality of the eternal high priest that the Church is associated in the action of the Eucharist, actualizing the priesthood which is hers by her unity with Christ's priesthood in the bond of the Spirit.[22]

Karl Rahner distinguishes, in a sacrament, the sacramental rite from the reality of grace signified by the rite. Applying this distinction to the Eucharist, he relates the priesthood of Christ and the ministerial

---

[21]   Maurice de la Taille, *The Mystery of Faith* II, trans. Joseph Carroll (New York, 1950[2]), p. 187.
[22]   Joseph M. Powers, *Eucharistic Theology* (New York, 1967), pp. 100–101.

priesthood to each other in a manner that recalls the visible and invisible priesthood formulated by Gabriel Biel:

> The question whether the Mass is a visible sacrifice (as the Council of
> Trent defined), lies on the plane of the liturgical rite itself, which is
> performed by men. On this plane, men are physically the directly op-
> erative and principal cause, even though morally and juridically they act
> only in virtue of a commission, so that on this plane, leaving the other
> still completely out of account, Christ is morally and juridically the
> *offerens principalis*. The question of Christ's saving action becoming pres-
> ent under this liturgical rite, however, concerns the sphere of the
> supernatural, invisible reality which is produced solely by God as the
> actually operative first cause.[23]

In making this presentation of the important features of the doctrine
of the priesthood from references to Catholic tradition, the intention
is not to give the impression that the teaching was always simple,
unified and balanced.[24] The main purpose has been to highlight those
features which were challenged by Luther's conception of the priesthood
of Christ and the priesthood of all Christians: that the offering of the
Mass is principally the sacrificial action of Christ as Eternal High Priest,
yet becomes the offering of his Body, the Church, through the instrumentality of a visible, ministerial priesthood. A more comprehensive
presentation would have to acknowledge, for example, that little attention had been given to elaborating on the priesthood of the laity
until the liturgical movement of this century. It would also have to
acknowledge that many exegetical problems remain in establishing the
basis of a ministerial priesthood.[25] Outside the Catholic tradition, some
admit of a scriptural basis for a ministerial priesthood; others deny it.[26]

---

[23] Rahner and Häussling, *The Celebration of the Eucharist*, p. 21.
[24] The following chapter will include the development of so-called "Mass-priests," and
       the abuses connected with private Masses.
[25] It is difficult, for instance, to find agreement on the meaning of *presbyteros* as used in
       the New Testament, to say nothing of the interdenominational differences regarding
       the origin of the episcopacy and the doctrine of apostolic succession.
[26] Hermann Sasse, *This Is My Body* (Minneapolis, 1959), p. 21, states: "There is no
       priesthood in the New Testament besides the High Priesthood of Christ and the uni-
       versal priesthood of His people. There is not the slightest indication that apostles,
       prophets, doctors, bishops, and other office-holders in the New Testament churches
       have a special dignity or office as priests beyond that which all Christians have." Max
       Thurian, *The One Bread* (New York, 1969), p. 63, acknowledges a special ministry

Inside the tradition, the validity of such a priesthood was affirmed again by the Second Vatican Council.[27] Without any doubt, the question of the ministry of the Church remains an important one in ecumenical dialogue. And to have examined the seminal differences at crucial periods of the history of the doctrine, for example, at the Reformation, can only clarify the issues involved in this dialogue.[28]

---

beyond that of all Christians: "Some Christians are ministers in the communion of Christ, namely, the deacon, pastor and episcopos (Jn. 13:17; Lk. 22:26–27; Jn. 10: 11; I Pet. 2:25, 5:1–14); they are chosen, called and ordained by Christ and given by him to the church to construct the Body of Christ . . . ."

[27] Cf. "Decree on the Ministry and Life of Priests," Ch. I, #2, in Austin Flannery, ed., *Vatican Council II: The Conciliar and Post Conciliar Documents* (Collegeville, 1975), pp. 864–66.

[28] For a specific and recent instance of such dialogue, cf. *Lutherans and Catholics in Dialogue* IV: *Eucharist and Ministry*. Published in 1970, this volume consists of position papers on various aspects of the ministry by American representatives of both traditions. The papers formed the basis of discussion at meetings held during a two-year period. As noted in the Introduction, the preceding volume in this series was *The Eucharist as Sacrifice*. The order of subject matter chosen for discussion by the representatives lends support to the order of presentation of this study.

CHAPTER VII
ABUSES IN THE MASS

oth as Augustinian friar and, later, as pastor of the City Church in Wittenberg, Luther had personal experience of abuses in the conception and celebration of the Mass. While he was sharply critical of these abuses, he contended that they could not be remedied without correcting the doctrine of the Mass itself. As long as the Mass was considered a sacrifice and a good work instead of a testament and gift from God, there could be no adequate solution to the problem of abuses.

There *were* abuses in the celebration of the Mass in the pre-Reformation era. No church historian, Catholic or Lutheran, questions this fact.[1] Exaggerated claims were made for attendance at Mass, claims which today would sound almost amusing were it not for the fact that they were sincerely believed by generations of the faithful. It was believed, for example, that one's digestion improved after having attended Mass. A person did not advance in age during the time he was present at Mass. He who heard Mass devoutly was assured of the remission of his sins and the reception of the sacraments of the Church at the moment of his death. If a pregnant woman gave birth to her

---

[1] There is a difference of opinion, however, as to whether these abuses also imply a defective doctrine of the Eucharist in this era. Francis Clark, *Eucharistic Sacrifice and the Reformation* (London, 1960[2]), p. 509, concludes his extensive examination of this question, primarily in the context of the English Reformation, with evidence of "a body of sound and traditional doctrine about the essentials of the Eucharistic sacrifice, common to all the schools of the time whatever their domestic disputes about lesser points." This position is strongly contested by John Jay Hughes, *Stewards of the Lord: A Reappraisal of Anglican Orders* (London, 1970), especially chapters 3 and 5.

child on the same day that she attended Mass, she would have an easy delivery. These and similar benefits appear on the lists of *fructus Missae* of the fourteenth and fifteenth centuries. Often, particular benefits were attributed to one of the apostles or to a Father of the Church for their formulation.[2] Although the theology of the day did not approve such exaggerated claims, they were able to flourish in devotional literature. The result was that people were encouraged to zealous attendance at Mass and looked upon this as a panacea for all their ills, spiritual and temporal.

As a consequence, the number of Masses increased. Votive Masses, offered for the wishes and intentions of the living and for the dead, were popular. Often a series of Masses—three, five, seven, as many as thirty—was requested for the same intention. What was really questionable in this practice was the implied assurance of unfailing results. Together with the increase in the number of Masses came an increase in the number of priests, some of whom derived their entire income from the stipends received in offering Masses.[3]

The manner of celebrating the Mass also left much to be desired at this time. The liturgy was mainly a liturgy for the clergy, with little participation by the people. Sacred music was professionalized, with an emphasis on polyphony. The occasional words of the priest addressed to the people were taken up and answered by the *schola cantorum*. The choir thus achieved a new prominence in the churches and in this respect the liturgy was enriched. But coincidentally, the liturgy in its deepest meaning was often neglected by the faithful; they became spectators rather than participants.[4]

Sacramental participation was also at a low ebb. Devotional piety placed greater emphasis on adoration of the Sacred Host than on its sacramental reception. To gaze upon the Host at the moment of the elevation in the Mass seemed more beneficial than to receive Communion.[5] An emphasis on the Real Presence took primacy over the sacrificial and sacramental dimensions of the Mass.[6]

---

[2]   Adolph Franz, *Die Messe im deutschen Mittelalter* (Freiburg i. Br., 1902), pp. 43–44.
[3]   Joseph Jungmann, *The Mass of the Roman Rite: Its Origins and Development* I, trans. Francis E. Brunner (New York, 1950), p. 130.
[4]   Cf. Robert E. McNally, *The Unreformed Church* (New York, 1965), p. 118.
[5]   Franz, *Die Messe im deutschen Mittelalter*, pp. 100–102.
[6]   McNally, *The Unreformed Church*, p. 124. Cf., also, on this point, Joseph Jungmann, "Liturgy on the Eve of the Reformation," *Worship* XXXIII (August–September 1959),

These were some of the chief abuses and false emphases connected with Mass-practice at the end of the Middle Ages and extending into the sixteenth century and even beyond. They were peculiar to the liturgical life of the Church at this period. Yet, the doctrine of the Mass as sacrifice, to which Luther attributed such abuses, was part of a constant, if not fully articulated, tradition going back to the primitive Church.

Joseph Jungmann finds that a sacrificial element is at least presupposed in some of the earliest documents referring to the Eucharist.[7] Some prominent Church Fathers speak of the Mass as a sacrifice. Augustine terms it the daily sacrifice of the Church, related to the sacrifice of the cross as a sacrament is related to that which is signified. John Chrysostom emphasizes that the Mass is one and the same with that of the cross. Other Fathers explain the efficacy of the Mass, dispensing to the living and the dead the grace of the unique sacrifice of Christ.[8] Drawing together these different emphases, we have a fairly comprehensive patristic doctrine, affirming the sacrificial nature of the Eucharist.[9]

---

5 11. In this article, Jungmann discusses the Mass abuses mentioned here but observes also that we may speak of a flowering of liturgical life on the eve of the Reformation, in the sense that the social life of the people was still part of a sacred order. The flowers, however, were "autumn flowers, late products of an ancient tradition" (*ibid.*, 5 1 3).

[7] In the *Didache*, for example, and in the writings of Ignatius of Antioch (Jungmann, *The Mass of the Roman Rite* I, p. 25). The New Testament evidence has been examined from this perspective by Tibor Horvath, *The Sacrificial Interpretation of Jesus' Achievement in the New Testament* (New York, 1979); the New Testament and patristic evidence (to Irenaeus of Lyon) by Helmut Moll, *Die Lehre von der Eucharistie als Opfer* (Köln, 1975), and also by Robert J. Daly, *Christian Sacrifice: The Judaeo-Christian Background before Origen* (Washington, 1978). Alasdair I. C. Heron, *Table and Tradition. Toward an Ecumenical Understanding of the Eucharist* (Philadelphia, 1983), also reviews the New Testament evidence on the Eucharist and gives a brief history of it through the Reformation. In a concluding section, he explores possible common ground between the Catholic and Reformed traditions regarding the Eucharist, pages 167–75 dealing with the sacrificial dimension. In another very interesting study, *Eucharist and Offering* (New York, 1986), liturgical historian Kenneth W. Stevenson examines the eucharistic prayers and hymns in the East and West from the metaphor of sacrifice as it is expressed in the elements of what he terms story, gift and response. Using this wider notion of sacrifice, Stevenson is able to discover a continuity of sacrificial emphasis in the rites extending from the primitive Church through history to the revised rites of the Christian churches today.

[8] M. Lepin, *L'Idée du sacrifice de la Messe d'après les Théologiens depuis l'origine jusqu'à nos jours* (Paris, 1926), p. 83.

[9] Franz summarizes the doctrine at the beginning of his work, *Die Messe im deutschen Mittelalter*, p. 4: "Nach der Lehre der Väter ist die Messe ein Opfer, das in unblutiger

The first monograph on the Eucharist did not appear in the tradition until the ninth century. This fact may be interpreted to mean that no serious challenge to the understood doctrine of the Eucharist arose before that time—no challenge that would call for its defence. The monograph, *De Corpore et Sanguine Domini* (831),[10] came from the pen of Paschasius Radbertus (c. 785–c. 860). As the title suggests, it dealt principally with the presence of Christ in the Eucharist. Radbertus taught that in the Mass the substance of bread and wine is changed into Christ's body and blood and, in fact, into the very flesh born of Mary which had suffered on the cross, was buried and rose again. The association of the historical body of Christ with Christ present in the Eucharist left Radbertus open to the accusation by his critics that his interpretation was overly crude and realistic. The subsequent discussion of his position contributed to a reaction in the opposite direction and to the first major challenge to the traditional doctrine of the Eucharist. In the eleventh century, Berengar of Tours (c. 999–1088) adopted a theory of the Eucharist as a mere sign or symbol. Through the consecration of the Mass, he taught, a conversion occurs, not of the eucharistic elements themselves, but of the sentiment of the believer with respect to them.[11]

There were few challenges to the doctrine of the Eucharist as sacrifice before the sixteenth century. One example, however, is the teaching of Peter de Bruys (d., c. 1140), considered to have been a priest deprived of his office who began itinerant preaching in southern France. He rejected infant baptism, the Mass, church buildings as special places of worship and prayer, the veneration of the cross and the efficacy of prayers for the deceased.[12] He and his followers were answered by Peter the Venerable (c. 1094–1156) in *Tractatus contra Petrobrusianos*. Peter's

---

Weise das Opfer des Kreuzes wirklich darstellt und seinen Wert und Nutzen aus dem letzteren nimmt. Dieses unblutige Opfer des Altares, in welchem sich Jesus Christus von neuem in geheimnisvoller Weise seinem himmlischen Vater darbringt, ist der Quell der reichsten Gnaden. An denselben nehmen nicht bloss die, welche den Leib des Herrn empfangen, teil, sondern auch—freilich in verschiedenem Masse—die der heiligen Handlung beiwohnenden Gläubigen, und auch andere, Lebende und Verstorbene."
10   J. P. Migne, ed., *Patrologia Latina* CXX, cols. 1267–1350.
11   Charles E. Sheedy, *The Eucharistic Controversy of the Eleventh Century* (Washington, 1947), pp. 102–107.
12   Cross and Livingstone, *The Oxford Dictionary of the Christian Church*, p. 1071.

arguments in defence of the Mass provide a brief compendium of the eucharistic doctrine for this period of history. He presents the Eucharist as a prolongation of the redemption of Christ, elaborating on three principal assertions: the Eucharist is the continuing presence of Christ in his Church; the Eucharist is the sacrifice of Christ himself, once offered voluntarily to the Father, now committed to the Church as her continual offering until Christ comes again; the Eucharist is the constant food of the faithful to nourish their spiritual life and to anticipate their future life with Christ in glory.[13]

By the time of Thomas Aquinas, then, some tracts had been written on the subject of the Eucharist. His contribution, while drawing upon patristic texts and the writings of preceding theologians, was to cast the traditional doctrine into a systematic form. Without an attempt to treat his teaching in detail, it may be noted, with regard to the present purpose of this study, that he affirms the Eucharist both as sacrament and as sacrifice:[14] that, as sacrifice, the Eucharist is the *imago repraesentativa* of the passion of Christ, of the true immolation of Christ;[15] and that this representation of the passion and immolation of Christ occurs in the consecration of bread and wine in the Mass.[16] By reason of these affirmations, one of Aquinas' definitions of sacrifice, which became popular (and mis-applied) in later tradition, is: a sacrifice is spoken of properly when something is done to that which is offered to God.[17]

---

[13] Migne, *Patrologia Latina* CLXXXIX, cols. 719–850; the section dealing with the defence of the Mass is found in cols. 787–819.

[14] *Summa Theologica*, III, q. 79, a. 5: "Dicendum quod hoc sacramentum simul est sacrificium et sacramentum; sed rationem sacrificii habet, inquantum offertur; rationem autem sacramenti, inquantum sumitur."

[15] *Ibid.*, III, q. 85, a. 1: "Celebratio autem huius sacramenti . . . imago quaedam est repraesentativa passionis Christi, quae est vera eius immolatio. Et ideo celebratio huius sacramenti dicitur Christi immolatio."

[16] *Ibid.*, III, q. 80, a. 12, ad 3: "Dicendum quod repraesentatio dominicae passionis agitur in ipsa consecratione huius sacramenti, in qua non debet corpus sine sanguine consecrari."

[17] *Ibid.*, IIa–IIae, q. 85, a. 3, ad 3: "sacrificia proprie dicuntur, quando circa res Deo oblatas aliquid fit," as when animals are slain or burned, food is consumed. In this context, Aquinas is distinguishing sacrifice from *oblation*: the latter refers to anything offered to God, even if nothing be done to it; hence, every sacrifice is an oblation, but not conversely. When this particular definition was applied univocally to the Eucharist, theologians of a later tradition discussed how immolation was verified in its celebration; cf. E. L. Mascall, *Corpus Christi: Essays on the Church and on the Eucharist* (London, 1960[4]), pp. 85–89.

Very little writing on the Mass as sacrifice is found in the fourteenth and fifteenth centuries,[18] although the controversy initiated by Berengar concerning the presence of Christ in the Eucharist still received some attention from the theologians. But in the sixteenth century, the issue of the sacrificial character of the Eucharist became vital and crucial. In the tracts which flourished on the subject, it is significant to observe that medieval doctrine influenced both reformers and apologists alike in one respect: the redemptive act of Christ is restricted almost exclusively to the passion and death of Christ. Consequently, the Eucharist, in being related during this period to Christ's redemptive act, is treated almost exclusively with reference to the passion and death of Christ.[19]

Given the existence of acknowledged abuses in the Mass in the pre-Reformation era, and given the testimony of a constant though not fully articulated tradition in the Church that the Mass is a sacrifice, it is possible to evaluate Luther's manner of correcting these abuses. His specific measures must be viewed in the perspective of his general approach to reform.

Luther's idea of reformation was not primarily and consciously a protest against papal and ecclesiastical abuses. He was aware of the distinction between the Church militant on earth and the triumphant, spotless Church in heaven and realized that the first would be plagued with abuses until the full manifestation of the Kingdom of God at the end of history.[20] Likewise, with reference to the Eucharist, Luther wished not merely to correct the abuses of the Mass, but to question and reject the doctrine, as he understood it, that gave rise to such abuses, a doctrine he felt was at variance with that contained in Holy Scripture. For him, the Mass stood in irreconcilable opposition to the act of redemption which Christ accomplished once for all by his death on the cross. Repetition of the Mass denied that Christ's atoning act is eternally valid and implied that God must be propitiated by continued sacrifices.[21] Had Luther set out to correct only the abuses of the

---

[18] Iserloh, having examined forty-six authors of this period who wrote commentaries on the Fourth Book of the *Sentences* of Peter Lombard, reports that not one of them treats of the Mass as a sacrifice. Meinhold and Iserloh, *Abendmahl und Opfer*, pp. 78–79.

[19] Cf. Dix, *The Shape of the Liturgy*, p. 623; Lepin, *L'Idée du sacrifice de la Messe*, p. 263. This particular focus will be treated more fully in the final chapter.

[20] Heiko Oberman, *Forerunners of the Reformation* (New York, 1966), pp. 9–10.

[21] Gustaf Aulén, *Eucharist and Sacrifice*, trans. Eric H. Wahlstrom (Philadelphia, 1958), pp. 82–83.

Mass, he would have been concerned with the moral and disciplinary reform of the Church; but he was concerned more radically with doctrinal reform, convinced that there could be no genuine moral reformation without a preceding reformation of doctrine.[22] His plea for reformation was not so much a demand for individual, clerical reform as a protest against the "man-made road to reformation" itself.[23]

To characterize Luther's approach to reform in still other terms, it could be said that his reform measures called directly and ultimately for changes more in the *structure* of the Church than in the *life* of the Church. Previous calls for reform focused on re-vitalizing the life of the Church. True and lasting reform would be effected by the lives of holy and dedicated people within the ranks of the Church. The instruments of reform were at hand; they needed only to be taken seriously. Thus, the reform of religious orders of men and women followed the pattern of a stricter observance of the primitive Rule of the founders. For the reform of the Church at large, there were the canons of the councils and papal decrees, which attempted to give people elaborations of the imperatives of the gospel and of the pattern of life received from Christ and the apostles.[24] Luther's call for reform was more sweeping and more radical: the abolition of convents and monasteries, the elimination of conciliar and papal decrees, the denial of a ministerial priesthood, the primacy of the pope, and so forth. His reform affected the dogma, the sacraments, the hierarchical constitution of the Church.[25] He believed that a good life came from good doctrine, a sound Church from sound dogma.

Now that Luther's orientation to doctrinal and structural reform has been described, the concrete reform measures he proposed for the Mass may now be examined more closely. At first, it might seem that Luther, as a liturgist, was conservative. He did not wish to introduce a completely new service, but to revise the rite of the Mass already in use so that it would be more expressive of the simple institution of the

---

[22] In its opening session, the Council of Trent faced the same problem of the proper approach to the reform of the Church. Should matters of doctrine or matters of discipline be given priority? The Council resolved the problem by deciding to consider doctrinal decrees and reform decrees in parallel. Cf. Hubert Jedin, *A History of the Council of Trent*, Vol. II, trans. Ernest Graf (St. Louis, 1957), pp. 29ff.
[23] Oberman, *Forerunners of the Reformation*, p. 10.
[24] Yves Congar, *Vraie et fausse réforme dans l'Eglise* (Paris, 1950), p. 357.
[25] *Ibid.*, p. 362.

Eucharist by Christ according to Scripture.[26] His aim was to restore the Mass to its original form in the primitive Church and to strip away the accretions of the centuries. Yet this revision and restoration involved a major liturgical change: the elimination of the Canon of the Mass. The prayers of the Canon refer to the Mass as a sacrifice and Luther wanted to repudiate any hint of this notion in his evangelical Mass. Accordingly, he called for the elimination of the Canon, except for the words of institution in his *Formula Missae* of 1523, and he supported his demand by a prayer-by-prayer critique of the Canon in *Vom Greuel der Stillmesse* of 1525.

As in other areas of reform, so also here Luther's yardstick of authentic doctrine was *sola scriptura*. The Scriptures taught that the death of Christ was the only sacrifice on which we can rely; yet the prayers of the Canon obscured this message by speaking about our sacrifices. Therefore, the Roman Canon, which some liturgists connect in origin with the Eucharistic Prayer of Hippolytus of the early third century,[27] must be abolished. Such a procedure to recapture the pure doctrine of Scripture by-passes, in my opinion, many centuries in which the liturgical life and the tradition of the Church enriched her understanding of the New Testament doctrine of the Eucharist. The interpretation of Scripture does not take place *in abstracto*, but is attendant upon the interplay between the life of the Church in an abiding tradition and academic exegesis. To interpret Scripture, therefore, without taking into account the liturgical tradition of the Church is to risk missing the full message of Scripture. The main difficulty with the Reformation principle of *sola scriptura* is, as Jaroslav Pelikan has observed, that the *scriptura* has never really been *sola!*[28]

Jerome Emser had criticized Luther on this very point in the sixteenth century. In responding to Luther's protest that the prayers of the Canon were mere additions by the Church, he suggests that the reformer is somewhat naive in having recourse to the Scriptures and expecting to find there the rite of the Mass or any other Christian rite.

---

[26] Luther D. Reed, *The Lutheran Liturgy* (Philadelphia, 1959), p. 72.
[27] *Ibid.*, p. 33. Reed, a Lutheran liturgist, states: "The Eucharistic Prayer (Anaphora) of Hippolytus gives us the earliest form of what later developed into the Canon of the Mass."
[28] Jaroslav Pelikan, "Luther and the Liturgy," in *More About Luther*, Vol. II (Decorah, Iowa, 1958), 50–51.

Christ did not set forth an order of celebration in instituting the Eucharist, nor a rite of administration in instituting any of the other sacraments. He left it to the Church, under the influence of the Holy Spirit and, therefore, in fidelity to scriptural evidence, to draw up such orders and rites.[29] In Luther's view, this liberality of Christ resulted in the use of the prayers and services composed by liturgists as a means of atonement for themselves and others. In the case of the Eucharist, this practice led to a perversion of the original intention of Christ and the only way in which it could be corrected was to adopt the liturgical principle that the closer the new order of service resembled what Christ said and did at the Last Supper, the more authentic it would be.

In effecting this liturgical reform, however, Luther shared with his fellow theologians of the sixteenth century certain deficiencies in historical perspective.[30] Liturgical research was in its infancy, and liturgical theology had not yet been born. The origins of individual ceremonies and of the Mass liturgies were generally unknown. Yet there were some theologians who claimed that entire liturgies could be traced back to the apostolic tradition.[31]

With respect to Luther's own knowledge of early Christian literature, there was a considerable gap between the writers of the New Testament and the earliest Church Fathers. He regarded Tertullian (d. 230) as the earliest writer in the Church after the apostles. Consequently, he did not really know the writers who later acquired the title, "Apostolic Fathers."[32] Similarly, he could not know the influence of some of these Fathers, especially Justin Martyr (c. 100–c. 165) and Hippolytus of Rome (c. 190–c. 236), on the formation of the Roman Canon.[33] In fact, he normally reckoned the "corruption" of eucharistic

---

[29] Emser, *Missae Christianorum, Corpus Catholicorum* XXVIII, p. 9: "Neque enim evangelium neque Christus ipse exactam mysteriorum suorum formam nobis tradidit, sed prima tantum rudimenta a spiritu sancto et ecclesia deinde absolvenda."

[30] "The lack of historical perspective, due to the mediaeval ignorance of history, was perhaps the greatest single contributory cause in the intellectual field of the sixteenth century break-up of christendom" (Dix, *The Shape of the Liturgy*, p. 627).

[31] Theisen, *Mass Liturgy and the Council of Trent*, pp. 112–13.

[32] Pelikan, *Luther the Expositor*, pp. 83–84.

[33] Cf. Jungmann, *The Mass of the Roman Rite* I, pp. 22–28. It is Jungmann's opinion that at least the core of the Roman Canon existed by the end of the fourth century (*ibid.*, p. 51).

doctrine by the introduction of the Canon prayers to have taken place around the seventh century.[34]

These limitations of historical perspective throw some light on why Luther considered the Canon prayers—and the doctrine implied in them—to be importations into the eucharistic liturgy by a later tradition of the Church. Nevertheless, his elimination of the Mass Canon was a drastic act, illustrating rather conclusively that Luther was interested primarily in doctrinal reform as the most effective way of correcting the abuses associated with the Mass. Unfortunately, he thereby set aside a prayer which originated in the early tradition of the Church and which bore witness to the presence in that tradition of the doctrine of the Mass as sacrifice. It was an action that is regretted by some Lutherans today as having robbed their liturgy of a certain historical and ecumenical character and as having relied too heavily upon the *verba* alone of the gospel message.[35]

The private Mass was one particular abuse that drew extensive criticism from Luther. After 1530, he wrote two tracts on this subject: *Von der Winkelmesse und Pfaffenweihe* in 1533 and *Die Disputation contra missam privatam* in 1536. Because of this attention, Luther's treatment of the private Mass deserves some comment as this chapter on abuses is concluded.

The term "private Mass" was used by medieval authors to describe "a Mass celebrated for its own sake, with no thought of anyone participating, a Mass where only the prescribed server is in attendance, or even if no one is present."[36] For Luther, the private Mass, like any other Mass, was an "abomination" because it was considered to be a sacrifice and a good work instead of a *testamentum* and a *beneficium*. But Luther had additional objections against the private Mass. In its celebration, the words of institution, which contain the promise of the testament, are not announced and proclaimed to the people; instead, the priest murmurs them to himself. This fault further militates against

---

34   Pelikan, *Luther the Expositor*, pp. 239–40.
35   Cf. Reed, *The Lutheran Liturgy*, p. 349. The author feels that this deficiency has been corrected by the *Common Liturgy*, drawn up for Lutherans in 1958 (*ibid.*, pp. 356–57). Subsequent liturgies were developed by the Inter-Lutheran Commission on Worship in 1978 (*Lutheran Book of Worship*) and by the Churches of the Missouri Synod in 1982 (*Lutheran Worship*).
36   Definition given by Jungmann, *The Mass of the Roman Rite* I, p. 215.

the Eucharist as *testamentum*. Again, in the celebration of the private Mass, only the priest communicates, except when a server is present and receives the sacrament. But since the Eucharist was instituted as food for the people, this fault further militates against it as a *beneficium* of God to his people.

In addition to these doctrinal considerations, Luther objected to the private Mass because it was not a practice of the early Church, but rather an invention of later tradition. He maintained that it was introduced by Pope Gregory the Great (590–604).[37] In this argument, Luther was not far from the mark. Contemporary research places the origin of the private Mass earlier than the time of Gregory, but still in the sixth century.[38] Whether the private Mass, especially the kind understood by the term in the sixteenth century, was in vogue in the earlier patristic age, is a debatable question.[39]

The celebration of Mass in private developed in the Church, according to Gregory Dix, as a result of two principal factors: the personal devotion of the presbyters and the piety of the faithful expressed in requests that Masses be offered for various intentions (votive Masses). As churches multiplied, presbyters became not just concelebrants with their bishop or deputies to celebrate the stational liturgy in his absence, but permanent delegates who were the normal celebrants for a congregation in a "parish church," which the bishop only occasionally visited. Once liturgy became part of the presbyter's office as such, the same devotional tendency that led to a daily corporate Eucharist for the communion of the laity and the daily celebration of the liturgy for various religious orders inevitably led the zealous presbyter to wish to celebrate daily. This desire was met more frequently and more easily when the presbyter simplified the liturgy and required only the assistance of one server to respond to the priest. Concurrent with this development was

---

[37]   *Die Disputation contra missam privatam*, WA 39[1], 141.

[38]   Jungmann, *The Mass of the Roman Rite* I, p. 218, says that about the turn of the sixth century, it was not unusual for a priest to read Mass for a deceased person on a series of days, with no one participating. Angelus Häussling, "Ursprünge der Privatmesse," *Stimmen der Zeit* CLXXVI (April 1965), 22, finds the first evidence of private Masses among the Celtic and Gallic Churches towards the end of the sixth century. Otto Nussbaum, *Kloster, Priestermönch und Privatmesse* (Bonn, 1961), pp. 139ff., likewise traces the practice to the Celtic monks of the sixth century.

[39]   Theisen, *Mass Liturgy and the Council of Trent*, p. 77.

the growing awareness among the laity that the celebration of the Eucharist was an act whereby Christ continued to bring all things under the rule of his Kingship. It was natural then to seek to bring themselves and the particular circumstances of their lives under this Kingship by entering into this act of Christ in some fashion. They therefore requested that Masses be offered for specific intentions, believing that, as members of Christ and of his Church, they would benefit from such requests even though they might be prevented by circumstances from being present at the eucharistic celebration.[40]

By the sixteenth century there were acknowledged abuses connected with the celebration of private Masses. Luther testifies from his own experience to the haste and lack of reverence with which these Masses were said, to the anticipation of guaranteed results on the part of the laity, and to the emergence of a special class of Mass-priests, devoted almost exclusively to saying private Masses and deriving their livelihood from the stipends received.[41] Such circumstances tended to discredit the practice of private Masses, and Luther was not alone in raising his voice against them. George Witzel (1501–1573), a liturgist and member of the Catholic party for reform, followed Luther in calling for the abolition of private Masses in a work on ecclesiastical concord published in 1539. For Witzel, the Mass was a *publica liturgia* to be participated in by the entire community. In his liturgical works, he tried to bring into focus the communal nature of the sacrifice and to demonstrate it as something to be participated in and understood by the laity.[42]

The Catholic apologists of the time defended the practice of the private Mass. In their eagerness, however, they generally erred from the historical point of view in attempting to prove its ancient and even apostolic origin. This deficiency aside, they were willing to recognize and correct the abuses of irreverence, superstition and avarice connected with the private Mass in order to retain it as a valid and legitimate

---

[40] Dix, *The Shape of the Liturgy*, pp. 593–94.
[41] Cf. Luther's final exhortation to priests in *Vom Missbrauch der Messe*, WA 8, 560; and his summary of objections to the private Mass in *Von der Winkelmesse und Pfaffenweihe*, WA 38, 225.
[42] John P. Dolan, *History of the Reformation. A Conciliatory Assessment of Opposite Views* (New York, 1965), pp. 376–81, summarizing Witzel's *Methodus Concordiae Ecclesiasticae*.

form of eucharistic celebration. The essence of the Mass is not impaired if the priest alone partakes of the sacrament, they argued.[43] Later, their defence of the private Mass would be officially supported by the Council of Trent. In a balanced statement indicating its preference that, at the celebration of the Eucharist, the faithful who are present should receive the sacrament, the Council also approves the private Mass as a legitimate form of celebration:

> The holy Council wishes indeed that at each Mass the faithful who are present should communicate, not only in spiritual desire but also by the sacramental partaking of the Eucharist, that thereby they might derive from this most holy sacrifice a more abundant fruit; if, however, that is not always done, it does not on that account condemn as private and illicit those Masses in which the priest alone communicates sacramentally, but rather approves and commends them, since these Masses also ought to be considered as truly common, partly because at them the people communicate spiritually and partly also because they are celebrated by a public minister of the Church, not for himself only but for all the faithful who belong to the body of Christ.[44]

Here, the Council explains how Masses, in which the priest alone communicates, are not strictly speaking "private" but "truly common." On similar theological grounds have such Masses been affirmed in subsequent Catholic tradition as legitimate forms of celebrating the Eucharist.[45] No sacrifice is ever offered to God except on the part of the whole

---

[43] Theisen, *Mass Liturgy and the Council of Trent*, p. 86.
[44] H. J. Schroeder, trans., *Canons and Decrees of the Council of Trent* (St. Louis, 1960), p. 147.
[45] Vatican II, *Constitution on the Sacred Liturgy*, Ch. I, #27, also indicates its preference for celebration of the Mass "in common" to that in which it is celebrated "by an individual and quasi-privately," even though "every Mass has of itself a public and social nature" (Flannery, *Vatican Council II*, p. 11). Nevertheless, in the context of concelebration, Ch. II, #57, the Council provides that "each priest shall always retain his right to celebrate Mass individually, though not at the same time in the same church as a concelebrated Mass . . ." (*ibid.*, p. 19). In 1965, Pope Paul VI emphasized more strongly than Vatican II the legitimacy of Masses celebrated individually, in his encyclical "Mysterium Fidei": "For even though a priest should offer Mass in private, that Mass is not something private; it is an act of Christ and of the Church. In offering this sacrifice, the Church learns to offer herself as a sacrifice for all. Moreover, for the salvation of the entire world she applies the single, boundless, redemptive power of the sacrifice of the cross. . . . Hence, although the very nature of the action ren-

Church. Hence, there is never such a thing as the private sacrifice of the priest; no matter how "private" it may be, the celebration of Mass is always a public act by a public minister on behalf of the whole Church, the Body of Christ.[46]

ders most appropriate the active participation of many of the faithful in the celebration of the Mass, nevertheless, that Mass is to be fully approved which, in conformity with the prescriptions and lawful traditions of the Church, a priest for a sufficient reason offers in private, that is, in the presence of no one except his server" (*Acta Apostolicae Sedis* LVII [October 1965], p. 761; translation from St. Paul Editions, Boston, Massachusetts). In view of this tradition, the observation of H. G. Haile, commenting on *Von der Winkelmesse*, is inaccurate: "As such, it eventually had a positive influence on the Roman church (which today disavows the private mass)" (*Luther: An Experiment in Biography*, p. 107).

[46] Cf. de la Taille, *The Mystery of Faith* II, p. 233.

CHAPTER VIII
DIVERGENCE ON RELATED DOCTRINES

uther's interest in the doctrinal reform of the Mass led him to fundamental assertions concerning the Eucharist that were at variance with previous Catholic teaching. The Mass, he concluded, is a testament, a promise of the remission of sins to all people, sealed by the external sign of the body and blood of Christ. It is neither a sacrifice nor a good work. What Luther held concerning the Eucharist is related to what he held concerning other doctrines of the Christian faith. Therefore, it is reasonable to expect that his assertions about the Eucharist also implied variations from previous tradition in other related doctrines. This chapter will examine the implications of Luther's eucharistic doctrine with respect to his conception of the atonement and the mediation of the grace of the atonement to us.

One of Luther's principal objections to the Mass was that, as a sacrifice, it stood in opposition to the one sacrifice of atonement in which Christ, by his death, offered himself once and for all for the sins of humanity. As an historical event, it was unique and could not be repeated. Moreover, since it was acceptable to God beyond all other sacrifices, and because of its intrinsic worth, no other sacrifice of atonement was necessary.[1] By this unrepeatable and all-sufficient sacrifice, Christ acquired for all time the remission of sins. But throughout time, the remission of sins would be granted to us through the means of grace, and especially in the observance of the Lord's Supper as a memorial of the atoning work of Christ.[2] In this manner, Luther conceives

---

[1]   Pelikan, *Luther the Expositor*, pp. 243–44.
[2]   Vajta, *Luther on Worship*, p. 59.

the atonement as an act of Christ wholly accomplished in the past, the effects of which may be appropriated by the faithful at any point in time. But he draws a sharp distinction between the single historical event of the sacrificial death upon the cross and the appropriation by the faithful of what was merited by that event.[3]

At the same time, Luther did not want to eliminate the element of sacrifice from Christian life and worship. It is just that the sacrifice found here is not an atoning sacrifice. In fact, because the need for an atoning sacrifice has been met by the work of Christ, the Church is free to introduce into its worship service those sacrifices which are more appropriate to our response in worship—sacrifices of thanksgiving and of praise.[4] In the sphere of Christian life, the death and resurrection of Christ are brought into the present through the lifelong struggle of the Christian against the devil, the world and his own flesh. The sacrifice entailed in this on-going struggle can be an offering in and with Christ, as the Christian tries through faith to conform his life to the life of Christ. Effecting this conformity is the Spirit, who always works to make Christ present to the Christian. The Holy Spirit is the mediating link between the glorified Christ and the Christian (and, on the broader plane, the Christian community).[5] Hence, the sacrifice of Christ, which took place once and cannot be repeated, lives on through the work of the Spirit in the reality of the Christian community.[6] But for Luther, this is the only way in which we may speak of Christ's atoning act as present.

In the celebration of the Eucharist, therefore, there is no question of the presence of the atoning act of Christ. The Eucharist is a memorial of that act, reminding the faithful of the atonement as a wholly past action, present only in the benefits now received from it. This conception of the atonement differed significantly from that which prevailed in the Catholic tradition previous to Luther. There, the atonement was viewed not merely as a past action but as a continuing reality. Moreover, it was in the celebration of the Eucharist that the atonement was believed to be made present in time—rendered present, not just

---

3   Meinhold and Iserloh, *Abendmahl und Opfer*, p. 67.
4   Pelikan, *Luther the Expositor*, p. 245.
5   Prenter, *Spiritus Creator*, pp. 25–26, 54.
6   Cf., also, Althaus, *The Theology of Martin Luther*, p. 315.

in its effects, but in the atoning act itself. The Eucharist was the point of contact in time between the atonement as an eternal and meta-historical event and its actualization at a particular moment within history.[7] To explain how the atonement was thus actualized and made present in the eucharistic celebration exercised the ingenuity of theological minds. It was as much a problem then as it is now.

Previously in this study, Aquinas' expression for the Eucharist, *imago representativa passionis Christi*, has been referred to.[8] In using this expression, he did not intend to describe the Eucharist as a mere mental representation of the passion of Christ. It is clear from his treatment that the passion of Christ is made present in some way, that the Eucharist, like the event of Calvary, is a sacrifice. There is but one victim: that which Christ offered and that which we offer. Since there is but one victim, there is but one sacrifice.[9] The altar, upon which the Eucharist is offered, is representative of the cross upon which Christ offered himself.[10] The priest who celebrates the Eucharist bears the image of Christ, in whose power he pronounces the words of consecration.[11] In the sacrifice of the Eucharist, one with the sacrifice of the cross, the victim and the priest are one and the same, Christ himself. The celebration of the Eucharist sets forth the one sacrifice of Christ, his act of atonement, at a particular point in space and time.

In a more contemporary formulation, the same doctrine is expressed in different terms. The sacrifice of the Mass is a *representatio sacrificii crucis* for these reasons: the liturgical rite itself, in the words of consecration and the duality of the elements, refers back to the sacrifice of the cross; *Christus passus* (whose suffering, as a personal and spiritual event, concerns the present even though the material, physical occurrence in which this event was realized is past) is really present under the sacramental elements. In this form, Christ is offered to the Father

---

[7]   Dix, *The Shape of the Liturgy*, p. 265. David W. Hay favours Dix's description of divine time as meta-history rather than the Greek notion of a "timeless now"; on the relation of divine time to our time and of the atonement to the celebration of the Eucharist, cf. his perceptive article, "Theology of Eucharist: The Church's Spiritual Sacrifice," in *National Bulletin on Liturgy*, Vol. XV, No. 82 (January–February 1982), especially 18–20.

[8]   *Summa Theologica*, III, q. 85, a. 1.

[9]   *Ibid.*, III, q. 85, a. 1, ad 1.

[10]   *Ibid.*, III, q. 85, a. 1, ad 2.

[11]   *Ibid.*, III, q. 85, a. 1, ad 3.

by the Church commissioned by him as the Christ who suffered and died. This offering takes place on two levels, that of the liturgical and ritual, accomplished in words and gestures, and that of the invisible and interior, accompanied by the worshipper's believing assent to the attitude of Christ's loving obedience to the Father.[12]

Why did Luther consistently look upon the atonement as an action completed in the past, over against a tradition that viewed it as an action continually actualized in the present? The basic reason is that Luther's understanding of the atonement itself differed from that of the Catholic tradition. Luther conceived of the atonement in essentially passive terms as a substitutionary suffering by Christ of the punishment of death under the wrath of God for the sins of the world.[13] Catholic tradition conceived of it in more active terms as a voluntary performance of a recompense by Christ to make up for the injustice and offence caused by sin.[14] In the latter instance, atonement is not so much the suffering of the punishment—death—as an act of satisfaction involving death.

There is recognizable here a similarity between these two conceptions of the atonement and the celebrated disjunction of St. Anselm (c. 1033–1109), *aut poena aut satisfactio*, which he proposed in devising his own explanation of the atonement in *Cur Deus Homo?*[15] It would not be accurate to align Luther and the Catholic tradition neatly with the respective members of Anselm's disjunction. Luther does make use

---

[12] As explained by Karl Rahner in *The Celebration of the Eucharist*, pp. 23–24.

[13] Wisløff, *The Gift of Communion*, pp. 110ff. This interpretation of Luther differs from that of Gustaf Aulén, *Christus Victor* (London, 1950; first published, 1931), and other interpreters who accept his thesis. Aulén develops what he calls the "classic" idea of the atonement: that it was God Himself who in Christ delivered humanity from the power of evil. Such an idea is the authentic interpretation of the atonement in the New Testament and the Fathers, according to Aulén, and was restored to the Christian tradition by Luther. For Wisløff's critique of Aulén, cf. pp. 122–24. The substitutionary interpretation of Luther's doctrine is found also in R. S. Franks, *The Work of Christ* (London, 1962), pp. 285–306, and especially pp. 285ff.; and in Louis Richard, *The Mystery of the Redemption* (Baltimore, Md., 1965), pp. 208–14.

[14] *Summa Theologica*, III, q. 48, a. 2.

[15] St. Anselm, *Cur Deus Homo?* in *Saint Anselm: Basic Writings*, trans. S. N. Deane, Bk. I, ch. 13: "Therefore the honor taken away (by the creature) must be repaid, or punishment must follow; otherwise, either God will not be just to himself, or he will be weak in respect to both parties; and this is impious even to think of."

of the expressions *satisfactio* and *meritum*;[16] and Catholic tradition was not always free from the substitution theory of the atonement.[17] Yet the emphasis of these two different conceptions of the atonement finds a parallel in Anselm's disjunction.[18]

The emphasis in Luther's conception of the atonement was upon the death of Christ. This death, as the punishment for sin, constituted the act of atonement, the supreme and unique sacrifice of Christ. Therefore, to speak of the sacrifice of Christ in the present time logically meant for Luther to speak of another death of Christ. This is impossible. Just as there is only one birth of Christ and one resurrection, there is one death.[19] Hence, the death of Christ, the act of atonement, the sacrifice of Christ, must remain a completed act of the past. On the other hand, the emphasis of the Catholic tradition's conception of the atonement as satisfaction focused rather upon the sacrificial disposition of Christ as being the essence of the atoning act: his obedient acceptance of whatever was necessary to obtain pardon for the offence of sin.[20] In this view, the passion and death of Christ constituted the concrete exterior expression of Christ's sacrificial disposition at the moment of the atonement.[21] But the sacrificial action and the sacrificial disposition are not identical. They stand in the same relation as constitutive sign and what is signified. Because they are not the same, they can each possess a different kind of temporal character: the original sacrificial action, as the material embodiment of the sacrificial disposition, may be already past; the sacrificial disposition, however, as an occurrence in the spiritual, personal domain of the God-man, can still

---

[16] Although Wisløff, *The Gift of Communion*, pp. 111–12, rightly indicates that Luther's meaning of these terms is not the same as their meaning in the Catholic tradition.

[17] Elements of the theory may be found in the writings of some of the Church Fathers, for example, Tertullian, Ambrose, Hilary; cf. Franks, *The Work of Christ*, pp. 8off. The influence of the theory was even greater in the post-Reformation Church, especially in the sermons of the French-Catholic orators of the seventeenth century; cf. Richard, *The Mystery of the Redemption*, pp. 237–39.

[18] Bernard Lonergan, *De Verbo Incarnato* (Rome, 1964), pp. 486–552, begins with Anselm's disjunction as a starting point in articulating a theory of vicarious satisfaction, using Scripture, the Fathers, conciliar statements, the opposing views of the Reformers including Luther, and especially the works of Aquinas, in advancing the thought of Anselm on the subject of the atonement.

[19] Cf. *Vom Missbrauch der Messe, WA* 8, 493.

[20] Lonergan, *De Verbo Incarnato*, pp. 507–10, 537–39.

[21] Cf. *Summa Theologica*, III, q. 14, a. 1, ad 1.

be present.[22] Consequently, the sacrificial disposition of Christ can be actualized in an appropriate constitutive sign, that is, in the visible, liturgical rite of the celebration of the Eucharist. In this way, the atonement is constantly being actualized in time.

These different views of the atonement and of its relation to time imply differences also in understanding and expressing the manner in which the grace of Christ is mediated to us. Since the atonement is a past event for Luther, he thought of its benefits as mediated primarily through faith in the promises of Christ, through faith aided by the exterior signs which Christ attached to his promises. The sacraments, baptism and the Eucharist, are the signs that elicit faith in the principal promises of Christ. This understanding of the mediation of grace de-emphasized the objective validity of the sacraments in comparison with the previous Catholic tradition, and placed a correspondingly greater emphasis on the role of faith. According to that tradition, grace is mediated not only by faith but also by the sacraments as efficacious signs of grace; that is, by the sacraments not only signifying the grace which is mediated but, in dependence upon the saving action of Christ as principal cause, causing the grace mediated. Such mediation is eminently verified in the Eucharist since, in the same tradition, it is the representation of the atonement itself, the source of all grace in the new dispensation. Biel describes this mediation in terms characteristic of his day:

> It was fitting that for all time there be for the human race a representative memorial of the Lord's passion which had been prefigured in so many ways in the Old Testament. Accordingly, in order to provide a perpetual and everlasting memorial of his most holy passion for the faithful, the Lord instituted this ineffable sacrament to his lasting memory, so that a sign of his accomplished redemption would not be lacking, a life-giving and efficacious sign by which the salvation gained by so many sufferings would be mediated to those redeemed and mystically prefigured for those to be redeemed.[23]

The Eucharist is a memorial of the Lord's redemptive act, but also an efficacious sign whereby redemptive grace is mediated to the faithful.

---

[22]   Rahner and Häussling, *The Celebration of the Eucharist*, pp. 16–17.

[23]   Biel, *Canonis Misse Expositio*, IV, Lect. 851, p. 104; my translation.

The other sacraments were also commonly considered instrumental causes of grace.[24]

The factors that led Luther to emphasize the role of faith in the mediation of grace are complex. An attempt will be made to delineate some of them, beginning with Luther's own personal experience of grace—an important factor which might easily be overlooked. Later in his career, Luther described a religious experience, the so-called "Tower Experience," which occurred sometime during the earlier years of his exegetical work.[25] Here, with sudden insight and clarity, he first came to understand "the righteousness of God," not in terms of his justice (active) but in terms of his mercy (passive); here, he perceived that our appropriate response is faith, and that this response represents a passive attitude before God. This religious experience, itself an experience of grace, occurred without being accompanied by any exterior, visible sign except for the passage of Scripture (Rom. 1:17) upon which Luther was meditating. This is how he describes the experience in the preface to his Latin works, published in 1545:

> At last, by the mercy of God, meditating day and night, I gave heed to the words namely, "In it the righteousness of God is revealed, as it is written, 'He who through faith is righteous shall live.'" There I began to understand that the righteousness of God is that by which the righteous lives by a gift of God, namely by faith. And this is the meaning: the righteousness of God is revealed by the gospel, namely, the passive righteousness with which merciful God justifies us by faith, as it is written, "He who through faith is righteous shall live." Here I felt that I was altogether born again and had entered paradise itself through open gates. There a totally other face of the entire Scripture showed itself to me. Thereupon I ran through the Scriptures from memory. I also found

---

[24] So the Council of Trent, in the context of the causes of justification, terms the sacrament of baptism. Cf. Denzinger and Schönmetzer, *Enchiridion Symbolorum*, #1529, p. 371.

[25] The date of the experience has been given as early as 1508 and as late as 1519. For periodic reviews of opinions, cf. Kenneth G. Hagen, "Changes in the Understanding of Luther: The Development of the Young Luther," *Theological Studies* XXIX (September 1968), 672–93; W.D.J. Cargill-Thompson, "The Problem of Luther's 'Tower Experience' and Its Place in his Intellectual Development," in *Studies in the Reformation: Luther to Hooker*, ed. C. W. Dugmore (London, 1980), 60–80; Marilyn J. Harran, *Luther on Conversion: The Early Years* (Ithaca, N.Y., 1983), pp. 174–88.

in other terms an analogy, as, the work of God, that is, what God does in us, the power of God, with which he makes us strong, the wisdom of God with which he makes us wise, the strength of God, the salvation of God, the glory of God.[26]

This was an overwhelming and expansive experience for Luther, one in which he saw how the manifold saving activity of God, specified by his attributes, reaches him directly through his simple response of faith, which is itself God's gift. It is understandable, therefore, that Luther would henceforth examine very closely any form of mediation of grace that relied upon the instrumentality of created means, material or human.

Yet, in his later theological development, Luther did not advocate a completely spiritualized view of the sacraments as means of grace. He acknowledged the sacraments as accompanied by exterior signs confirming the promise contained in the sacrament and inviting the response of faith.[27] But were these signs mere sign-posts for Luther, or did he consider them as having some intrinsic value in the mediation of grace? Certainly, in his earlier controversial tracts in the years 1519–1524, he assigned greater importance to the words of promise in the Eucharist than to the sign of the sacrament.[28] During the same period, he saw a parallel between the signs of the Old Testament and the sacraments of the New: both were attached to promises that elicited a faith response; in fact, through the promises a line of continuity was established between the Testaments because all of the ancient promises found their fulfillment in the promise and testament of Christ.[29] Yet the similarity of function between the signs of the two Testaments

---

[26]   *Vorrede Luthers zum ersten Bande der Gesamtausgaben seiner lateinischen Schriften*, WA 54, 186; *LW* 34, 337.

[27]   Jaroslav Pelikan, "The Theology of the Means of Grace," *Accents in Luther's Theology: Essays in Commemoration of the 450th Anniversary of the Reformation*, ed. H. Kadai (St. Louis, 1967), esp. 134–38.

[28]   *Ein Sermon von dem neuen Testament*, WA 6, 363: "Also sehen wir, das das beste unnd gröste stück aller sacrament und der mesz sein die wort und gelubd gottis . . . ." Cf. Wisløff, *The Gift of Communion*, pp. 26–27. Prenter, *Spiritus Creator*, pp. 142–43, considers that Luther's emphasis on the promise at this stage "does not mean a spiritualizing of the idea of the sacrament but a sacramentalization of the message."

[29]   Cf. *De captivitate Babylonica*, WA 6, 514, 517–18.

depreciates, I think, the value of the sacramental signs of the New Testament because the signs of the Old Testament did not differ from other natural signs of creation except for the fact that they were associated with a divine promise.[30]

After 1526, however, Luther's appreciation of the objective value of the sacramental sign increases. In his controversy with the Swiss Reformers, he had defended the reality of Christ's presence in the sign of the Eucharist. Aided by a renewed study of the Fathers, he now speaks of the elements no longer as signs or pledges, but as direct channels of divine power.[31] Consequently, a fair interpretation of Luther's assessment of sacramental signs in the mediation of grace must take account of this change of emphasis between his earlier and later writings. Of course, the prominent role he assigned in this area to the Holy Spirit throughout his development must be acknowledged: as a present reality, the Spirit is the agent by which Christ comes out of the grave of history and becomes truly present. In his presence we are moved to the constant prayer of faith and to acts of love towards our neighbour.[32]

The weakness in the Catholic conception of the mediation of grace at the time was that excessive emphasis was placed on the efficacy of the sacrament itself. By the mere performance of the external rite, by the mere reception of the sacrament, *ex opere operato*, grace would be conferred. The tendency was to an almost superstitious reliance on the power (*virtus*) of the sacrament as a rite, to the neglect of the subjective dispositions of the recipient. It was this dangerous tendency that Luther so often confronted in the scramble for indulgences and the clamour for series of Masses; it prompted him to undercut the mediation of what he considered "human works" by stressing the role of faith.

If this was the interpretation that could rightly be given the popular piety of the period, there is nevertheless evidence also of continuing orthodox doctrine which, in time, would correct these false emphases.

---

[30] Congar, *Vraie et fausse réforme*, p. 406.

[31] Brilioth, *Eucharistic Faith and Practice*, pp. 106–107. Cf., also, *Der Grosse Katechismus* (1529), WA 30[1], 54, and later, *Kaspar Crucigers Sommerpostille* (1544), WA 21, 536, both references linking the work of the Spirit with the sign of water in baptism.

[32] The role of the Spirit according to Luther, as described by Prenter, *Spiritus Creator*, p. 171.

For example, as Cajetan succinctly explained the Catholic doctrine in 1510, the *opus* of the expression *ex opere operato*, when used with reference to the Mass, refers to the *passio Christi*. Considered in itself, this *opus* is infinite; considered as applied to the faithful, this *opus* has a limited effect "according to the measure of devotion of those offering [the Mass] or of those for whom it is offered."[33] In other words, the celebration of Mass (and derivatively, the reception of a sacrament, the performance of a good work) does not have an automatic or unlimited effect; rather, the effect, originating with the *opus Christi*, depends also upon the dispositions of those who stand to benefit from the Mass. Substantially the same doctrine was affirmed by the Council of Trent.[34]

Luther's personal experience of grace, his understanding from the Scriptures of how grace is communicated, his acquaintance with exaggerated emphases on the exterior means of grace—these were some of the factors that led him to de-emphasize the objective validity of the sacraments in the mediation of grace. Operative as well in working out this position were, I think, certain principles of nominalist philosophy which functioned as presuppositions in Luther's theological study. We know that he was familiar with Biel's *Canonis Misse Expositio*,[35] but the influence in question here comes more directly from William of Occam himself (c. 1300–c. 1349) and Pierre D'Ailly (1350–1420). Luther studied the works of Occam, the father of nominalism, and D'Ailly, his disciple, in the period 1507–1508.[36]

---

33 Cajetan, *De missae celebratione, Opuscula Omnia*, t. II, tr. 3, p. 147; my translation; J. Rivière, "Affirmations catholiques en face de la Réforme," *Dictionnaire de Théologie Catholique* X, 1, col. 1106, cites evidence of similar doctrine from the Catholic apologists.

34 At the conclusion of its section on the causes of justification, the decree on this subject reads: "Finally, the single formal cause is the justice of God, not that by which He Himself is just, but that by which He makes us just, that, namely, with which we, being endowed by Him, are renewed in the spirit of our mind (Eph. 4:23), and not only are we reputed but we are truly called and are just, receiving justice within us, each one according to his own measure, which the Holy Ghost distributes to everyone as He wills (I Cor. 12:11), and according to each one's disposition and cooperation" (Schroeder, *Canons and Decrees of the Council of Trent*, p. 33).

35 Cf. *supra*, p. 78, n. 21. Lortz, *The Reformation*, I, p. 444, believes the content of the *Expositio* to be largely non-Occamist. Further, Franz, *Die Messe im deutschen Mittelalter*, p. 553, provides the interesting testimony that the *Expositio* is not entirely original with Biel since about three-fourths of the work can be traced to a similar treatise by a certain Egeling Becker von Braunschweig (d. 1481).

36 Heinrich Boehmer, *Road to Reformation*, trans. John W. Doberstein and Theodore G. Tappert (Philadelphia, 1946), pp. 44–45. According to Boehmer, there is a lack of

In general, nominalist philosophy, when applied to sacramental theology, divorces the sacraments from the mediation of grace. Sacraments are not the causes of grace in any sense; they are merely the conditions, the occasions upon which God communicates his grace directly. Exteriorly and visibly, they are the arbitrary signs designated by Christ as the occasions for communicating God's grace—"arbitrary" signs, in the sense that other signs would have fulfilled the same function.[37] More specifically, the following nominalist principles would seem, in view of the discussion so far in this chapter, to have been especially operative in Luther's development:

(1) The will of God, revealed most clearly in the Scriptures, is the sole determinant cause of everything that happens; hence, secondary causality is negligible.[38] On the basis of this principle, then, we can understand Luther's solicitude in searching the Scriptures for those instances in which Christ made a promise of grace to which he attached a particular sign. Finding only two instances to verify these conditions, Luther logically concluded that there were only two sacraments, baptism and the Eucharist. Further, from the corollary of this principle it becomes clear how he could not regard these two sacraments as secondary, instrumental causes of grace.
(2) Since secondary causality is negligible, human beings have no causal atoning grace in themselves. Good works are irrelevant to salvation. In a world in which God is the sole cause of grace, the only response possible for us is one of complete self-abnegation and obeisance, a filial trust in the power of Almighty God. Realizing our own powerlessness and nothingness, we must wait upon the grace of God.[39] This conception of the God–human relationship fits very well with Luther's de-

evidence concerning whether Luther had the opportunity to study Aquinas or Scotus at this time. In any case, Occam, D'Ailly and Biel would be the "moderns" for him and undoubtedly more palatable. The extent of their influence on Luther continues to be researched: cf., for example, Heiko Oberman, "Headwaters of the Reformation: Initia Lutheri—Initia Reformationis," in *Luther and the Dawn of the Modern Era*, ed. H. Oberman (Leiden, 1974), esp. 54–69; Ozment, *The Age of Reform, 1250–1550*, pp. 55–63, 233–39.
37 Meinhold and Iserloh, *Abendmahl und Opfer*, p. 82.
38 P. Linwood Urban, Jr., *The Will of God: A Study of the Origin and Development of Nominalism and Its Influence upon the Reformation* (New York, 1959), p. 6.
39 *Ibid.*, p. 48, for the Moslem expression of this doctrine; related to Luther, pp. 156–58.

scription of his "Tower Experience": how he becomes just by the passive acceptance through faith of God's mercy.[40]

(3) Essence is existence and existence, essence; there is no real distinction between the two. A corollary of this principle is the singularity of reality: the link between two singulars can only be one of similarity and not of identity.[41] These presuppositions throw light upon Luther's inability to see the atonement as anything but a past event, and his inability to grasp the unity of the eucharistic offering and the offering of Christ on Calvary as one of essential identity through a form of sacrifice, where Christ's is the true sacrifice and each Eucharist is a manifestation of that sacrifice. From a nominalist perspective, the Eucharist is not the same sacrifice but another of the same kind; if it is to be considered a sacrifice, it can only be a repetition of the sacrifice of the cross.

Given his conception of the atonement as a past event, and his emphasis on faith in the mediation of grace with an accompanying reluctance to concede any effective instrumentality to external means of grace, Luther differed from Catholic tradition in thereby de-emphasizing the incarnational character of the Church. According to this, the Church, as the Body of Christ, mediates to the world the divine life of grace which flows from Christ, her Head. In this role, the Church is a perpetual extension of Christ's Incarnation. Her members receive the grace of salvation not only for the remission of sins but to be regenerated inwardly; living the life of Christ, they share actively in the on-going work of redemption. Even the powers of sanctification have been entrusted by Christ to the members of his Church: baptized and ordained members, as ministers of the sacraments, mediate to others the benefits of Christ's all-sufficient work of salvation.[42] Just as these

---

[40] The same conception likewise suits Luther's description of the process of conversion in *Vom Missbrauch der Messe*, WA 8, 552–53: "Die weyl der mensch ynn sunden geborn und entpfangen wirt und eyn kind des tzorns ist, szo kan er nichts denn sundigen und teglich mehr und mehr ynn gotts tzorn fallen, bisz szo lang er hort und gleubt, das Christus seyn heylandt uund fur yhn gestorben sey, auff das er yhn von seynen sunden erlost. Durch disz horen krumpt der geyst gotts yn seyn hertz und wirt mit gotts gnad und lieb durch gossen, das er gott liebet, seynen namen preyst und heyliget, feyrt und helt still uund lest gott ynn yhm seyn eygen werck wircken."
[41] Urban, *The Will of God*, p. 105.
[42] Cf. Clark, *Eucharistic Sacrifice*, p. 103.

are saved "in" and "through" Christ, they are saved "in" and "through" the Church. Luther admits of salvation "in" but not "through" the Church.

This conception of the nature of the Church and the role of its members is related to the Incarnation of Christ. Just as the Incarnation is the visible manifestation of God, whom no one has ever seen, so also the Church through visible sacraments and a visible sacerdotal ministry embodies the invisible working of divine grace throughout time until the end of time. For Luther, the Incarnation itself is conceived of in terms of the central fact of salvation, the passion and death of Christ. God made a testament with his people, a testament foreshadowed in the promises of the Old Testament and to be fulfilled in Christ. Where there is a testament, however, the death of the testator must of necessity occur (Heb. 9:16). But God could not die unless he became human. Hence, it was necessary that the Son of God become human in order that he might die and validate God's testament. The Incarnation and the death of Christ are both implied in the idea of testament.[43]

In Catholic tradition, on the other hand, the Incarnation was affirmed as being the foundation of the redemption and restoration of fallen humanity. The Son of God, in assuming human nature, had united the human to the divine, and a totally new relationship had arisen between God and humankind. Athanasius and Augustine had expressed this positive value of the Incarnation by saying that God became human in order that we might become divine.[44] In the *de facto* order of salvation, this relationship was effectively sealed and ratified by the passion, death and resurrection of Christ. The value of the Incarnation, therefore, is not independent of the atoning act of Christ. Yet, since it is not merely *ad passionem Christi*, the Incarnation, *post passionem*, retains its value: as the paradigm of the *way* of salvation, it indicates that the normal way to God leads through visible realities to those that are invisible. The mystery of the Church, with its sacraments and sacerdotal ministry, forms the counterpart of the Incarnation.[45] The implications of Luther's view of the atonement and of the mediation of grace suggest, in con-

---

[43]   Cf. *De captivitate Babylonica*, WA 6, 514.
[44]   W. H. Van de Pol, *The Christian Dilemma*, trans. G. Van Hall (London, 1952), p. 71.
[45]   *Ibid.*, p. 72.

trast, a conception of the Church that is more spiritual and less incarnational. For Luther, the atonement is Christ's all-sufficient act of reconciliation in the past, the effects of which are mediated to us through faith.

This discussion of differences between Luther and the Catholic tradition with respect to doctrines related to the Eucharist has ultimately led to the expression of a difference in the affirmation of the Incarnation.[46] It should be noted here that the orthodoxy of Luther's christology itself is not in question.[47] In fact, during the controversy concerning the Real Presence, Luther maintained the true humanity of Christ against the emphasis on his transcendence by Zwingli.[48] And the discussion of Luther's christology has greater relevance to this controversy.[49] Concern here has been rather with Luther's reluctance to affirm the extension of the Incarnation in the life and worship of the Church throughout history. This aspect of the Incarnation involves areas of doctrine relevant to the subject of this study: the nature of the atonement and the mediation of grace. In these areas there are significant differences between Luther and Catholic tradition: the atonement is not just a past event but an on-going reality; the grace of the atonement is mediated through external, visible signs from the created world and not only by the interior disposition of faith. The differences in these areas of doctrine are related in turn to a difference in the understanding of the Eucharist: for Luther, excluding its sacrificial dimension, the Eucharist is an abiding testament of the grace of the atonement offered to us; for Catholic tradition, retaining its sacrificial dimension, the Eucharist is a re-presentation of the atoning act itself.

---

[46] This difference, both for Luther and subsequent Lutheran and Catholic theologians, has been well explored by Averbeck, *Der Opfercharakter des Abendmahls in der neueren evangelischen Theologie*, esp. pp. 787–805.

[47] So also is the conclusion of Ian Siggins in his study of Luther's christology, *Martin Luther's Doctrine of Christ* (New Haven, Conn., 1970), p. 227.

[48] Cf. Brilioth, *Eucharistic Faith and Practice*, pp. 107–108.

[49] The position one takes on the Real Presence indicates whether one stresses the transcendence of the glorified Christ in heaven or the immanence of his presence under the material and temporal conditions of this world; both attributes relate to the divinity and humanity of the God-man. Cf. Meinhold and Iserloh, *Abendmahl und Opfer*, pp. 43–44; Prenter, *Spiritus Creator*, p. 158.

CHAPTER IX
AREAS OF AGREEMENT, THEN AND NOW

lthough Luther's doctrine of the Eucharist differed fundamentally from that of Catholic tradition and implied differences in understanding other doctrines related to the Eucharist, there were areas of agreement that ought not to be overlooked in examining these differences. Both parties affirmed that there is only one sacrifice of the New Testament, the unique and all-sufficient sacrifice of Christ.[1] Both parties affirmed that there is only one priesthood of the New Testament, the priesthood of Christ, though they differed in explaining how the office of priest is shared and exercised by members of the Church.[2] Finally, both parties considered the celebration of the Eucharist as a sacrifice of praise and thanksgiving, a rite in which the faithful were called upon to make an offering of themselves in union with the offering of Christ commemorated in the Eucharist.

Agreement on these points was obscured at the time by the lack of a well-defined and formulated theology of the Eucharist,[3] and this condition was especially true in the case of the affirmation of a single

---

[1] Luther scrupulously safeguarded this affirmation; for the consensus of Catholic opinion, cf. Clark, *Eucharistic Sacrifice*, pp. 93–94, ##ii, iv, vi.

[2] Luther found scriptural evidence only for the common priesthood of all baptized Christians; Catholic tradition maintained, in addition, the validity of an ordained, ministerial priesthood.

[3] "Von einer Theologie des Messopfers kann nicht gesprochen werden, wenn wir unter Theologie eine systematische und von den eignen Grundlagen her entwickelte Darstellung der katholischen Lehre und eine einigermassen geleistete Aufarbeitung der strittigen Probleme verstehen" (Iserloh, *Der Kampf um die Messe*, p. 56).

sacrifice. Luther was convinced that any affirmation of the Mass as a sacrifice involved a repetition of Christ's sacrifice on Calvary in every Mass. The Catholic apologists, many of whom maintained the virtual identity of Christ's sacrifice on Calvary and in the Mass,[4] were apparently not able to explain their position to Luther's satisfaction.[5] In the atmosphere of charge and counter-charge, there was little chance of reaching common understanding. But a more fundamental reason for the lack of understanding was the fact that both Luther and his Catholic apologists inherited from medieval theology the basic equation, "sacrifice = death."[6] Applied to Christ's sacrifice, this equation meant that the essential event of his atoning sacrifice was his death, and the Eucharist, in being considered a sacrifice, was related primarily to that death. It was incomprehensible to Luther how the historical event of Christ's death could be repeated in the celebration of the Eucharist; the Catholic apologists, with differing explanations, attempted and generally failed to show that his death could be made present in a different form in the Eucharist. The result was an impasse blocking any real meeting of minds.

Even within this restricted perspective, there was no common and adequate definition of sacrifice that could have served as a firm basis for discussion. This deficiency was likewise inherited from medieval theology. Aquinas himself provided different definitions according to the aspect of sacrifice he wished to stress.[7] Catholic apologists made use of the definitions of the medieval theologians, and of the Fathers as well, in formulating their own definitions.[8] The result, while gen-

---

[4] Cf. *ibid.*, pp. 17, 19, for the affirmation of this identity by Thomas Murner (1469–1537); pp. 42–43, by Kaspar Schatzgeyer (1463–1527); p. 49, by Johannes Mensing (d., c. 1541). More extensively on Schatzgeyer, cf. Kaspar Schatzgeyer, *Schriften zur Verteidigung der Messe*, eds., with introductions, Erwin Iserloh and Peter Fabisch (Münster, 1984), esp. pp. 199–347.

[5] *Ibid.*, p. 59.

[6] According to F.C.N. Hicks, *The Fullness of Sacrifice* (London, 1953), pp. 311–12. Cf., also, Clark, *Eucharistic Sacrifice*, pp. 383ff.; Jungmann, *The Mass of the Roman Rite* I, p. 177.

[7] For example, to stress immolation: "Sacrificia proprie dicuntur quando circa res Deo oblatas aliquid fit" (*Summa Theologica*, IIa–IIae, q. 85, a. 3, ad 3). To stress propitiation: "Sacrificium proprie dicitur aliquid factum in honorem Deo debitum ad eum placandum" (*ibid.*, III, q. 48, a. 3).

[8] Cf. Rivière, "Affirmations catholiques," *Dictionnaire de Théologie Catholique* X, 1, cols. 1106–1108.

erally accurate and rich in exploring the dimensions of the subject, failed to furnish a definition of sacrifice, at once essential and comprehensive, which would meet the demands of the controversy of that time.[9]

The Council of Trent did not make any significant contribution to solving this problem. Although it described the Mass as a *verum et proprium sacrificium*, it did not offer a definition of such a sacrifice.[10] Consequently, the post-Tridentine theologians set to work to explain the meaning of this phrase and to show how their explanation applied to the sacrifice of the Mass. Taking their cue from certain definitions of Aquinas and Cajetan,[11] many theologians were inclined to hold that some physical modification of the victim was essential to sacrifice. This accent on the immolation aspect of sacrifice led to theological explanations of the Mass that sought to demonstrate how the "destructive" sacrificial activity was verified in the Mass.[12]

According to the interpretation of F.C.N. Hicks,[13] this line of investigation was predominant in theological discussion of the sacrifice of the Mass until the nineteenth century. At that time, as a result of research into the history of early religion, sacrifice, and liturgy and in particular of Old Testament sacrifice, the notion of sacrifice was greatly expanded. The death of the victim was only one stage of the sacrifice as a whole. Other significant stages included: the identifica-

---

[9] Lepin, *L'Idée du sacrifice de la Messe*, p. 291.

[10] Denzinger and Schönmetzer, *Enchiridion Symbolorum*, #1751, p. 411. This deficiency of the Council may only be supplied by contemporary theological research according to Erwin Iserloh, "Luther and the Council of Trent," *Catholic Historical Review* LXIX (October 1983), 574–75; Theodor Schneider, "Opfer Jesu Christi und der Kirche: zum Verständnis der Aussagen des Konzils von Trient," *Catholica* XXXI (1977), 54, observes that we are perhaps fortunate that Trent did not formulate a definition of the sacrifice of the Mass at that time. The Council did state that the sacrifice of the Mass is *propitiatory* for the living and the dead (*Enchiridion*, ##1743, 1753). For this discussion and its bearing on contemporary ecumenical discussions, cf. the very thorough study of David N. Power, *The Sacrifice We Offer. The Tridentine Dogma and Its Reinterpretation* (New York, 1987).

[11] Following Aquinas' definition, which described sacrificial action *circa res oblatas*, Cajetan stressed the *status immolatitius* of Christ in the eucharistic sacrifice. Cf. *De missae sacrificio, Opuscula Omnia*, t. III, tr. 10, p. 286; Wicks, *Cajetan Responds*, p. 192.

[12] Jungmann, *The Mass of the Roman Rite* I, pp. 184ff.; cf. *supra*, p. 113, n. 17.

[13] Outlined briefly in a memorandum to a report, *The Second World Conference on Faith and Order*, ed. Leonard Hodgson (New York, 1938), pp. 326–27.

tion of the sinner with the victim; the presentation to God of the blood of the victim, symbolizing its surrendered life, and his acceptance of it; the consumption of the body of the victim, either by fire or in a common meal. In the light of these stages, many aspects of the atoning work of Christ, besides his actual death, took on a sacrificial dimension: his incarnation, by which he became one with sinful humanity; his priesthood, by which he presented the blood of his own self-oblation to the Father (Heb. 9:12); his resurrection and ascension, by which his sacrifice was accepted by the Father who glorified and exalted his Son.[14] Consequently, the eucharistic sacrifice, in re-presenting the integral atoning work of Christ, commemorates—from the preparation of the gifts of bread and wine through the Communion—not just his death but the sacrificial dimensions of these other mysteries of his life as well.

This expanded notion of sacrifice was carried into the present century as research continued on the history and nature of sacrifice. The result has been a renewed interest in the element of sacrifice in the Eucharist, even by non-Catholic theologians. The evidence for this interest is most easily documented, on an official level, by the reports of successive World Conferences on Faith and Order.

Meeting in Edinburgh in 1937, the Second World Conference clearly reflected the new perspectives of sacrifice in its statement on the sacrifice of Christ: "If sacrifice is understood as it was by Our Lord and His followers and in the early Church, it includes, not His death only, but the obedience of His earthly ministry, and His risen and ascended life, in which He still does His Father's will and ever lives to make intercession for us."[15] Although such a sacrifice can never be repeated, according to the Conference, it is proclaimed and set forth in the eucharistic action of the whole Church.

At Lund in 1952, the delegates to the Third World Conference found that they were able to reach an unexpected measure of understanding on the problem of the sacrificial element of the Eucharist. Their report, like that of the Second Conference, assumes a broad meaning of sacrifice: "Our Lord Jesus Christ in all His life on earth and chiefly in His death and resurrection has overcome the powers of darkness."[16]

---

[14] *Ibid.*, p. 327.
[15] *Ibid.*, p. 244.
[16] Oliver S. Tomkins, ed., *The Third World Conference on Faith and Order* (London, 1953), p. 42.

The death of Christ itself was considered by the delegates not so much in terms of the destruction of physical life but as an act of perfect obedience to the Father in atonement for the sins of the world. Concerning the relation of worship in the Eucharist to Christ's continual intercession in heaven, the delegates had greater differences, some allowing that in communion with the crucified and risen Lord they only offer a sacrifice of praise and thanksgiving and obedient service, others going so far as to say that in the Eucharist Christ as High Priest unites the oblation made by his body, the Church, with his own sacrifice, taking up its adoration into the *Sanctus* of the company of heaven.[17]

The Fourth World Conference on Faith and Order was held in Montreal in 1963. Its statement on the Eucharist contained a definite sacrificial emphasis: "Despite many disagreements regarding Holy Communion and despite the desire of many for a fuller statement, we are drawn at least to agree that the Lord's Supper, a gift of God to his Church, is a sacrament of the presence of the crucified and glorified Christ until he come, and a means whereby the sacrifice of the cross, which we proclaim, is operative within the Church."[18] Members of the Church, the statement explains, participate in this sacrament by offering to the Father their praise, thanksgiving and intercession, in union with Christ, their High Priest and Intercessor. With contrite hearts, they also offer up themselves as a living and holy sacrifice.[19]

Thus, in the discussion of the delegates to these Conferences on Faith and Order, the sacrifice of Christ is no longer restricted to his death, but refers as well to his life on earth and his life in glory. At the same time, the unrepeatable character of Christ's atoning act is consistently affirmed. Does it then follow that every event in the mystery of Christ's life to which the notion "sacrifice" pertains is also unrepeatable? The Fourth World Conference said as much: what God did in the incarnation, life, death, resurrection and ascension of Christ, he does not do again. The events are unique; they cannot be repeated, extended or continued.[20] On the other hand, there is an increasing reluctance in the Conference statements to regard the Eucharist as a mere recalling

---

[17] *Ibid.*, pp. 42–43.
[18] P. C. Rodger and Lucas Fischer, eds., *The Fourth World Conference on Faith and Order* (New York, 1964), p. 73.
[19] *Ibid.*, pp. 73–74.
[20] *Ibid.*, p. 73.

of a past event.[21] The increased emphasis on how the people participate
in the celebration of the sacrament, the references to some of the saving
acts of Christ, especially his high priestly intercession, as a present
activity, connote involvement in a present reality.

Dialogue on the Eucharist, as well as on baptism and the ordained
ministry, continued to engage the Faith and Order Commission
through the 1970s: at Accra (1974) and Bangalore (1978). The Fifth
World Council Assembly in Nairobi (1975) authorized the distribution
to the member churches of the text prepared on these subjects, inviting
suggestions for further revision. The responses were considered and the
text revised at Lima in 1982, and the Faith and Order Commission
unanimously voted upon a final document.[22]

This document, in the section on "The Meaning of the Eucharist,"
builds upon previous statements of agreement and also reflects new
formulations expressing a greater convergence of understanding. The
Eucharist "is the memorial of the crucified and risen Christ, i.e. the
living and effective sign of his sacrifice, accomplished once and for all
on the cross and still operative on behalf of all humankind." It "is the
sacrament of the unique sacrifice of Christ, who ever lives to make
intercession for us." Once again, the document stresses that Christ's
saving events—his life, death, resurrection and ascension—are unrepeatable; these events "are unique and can neither be repeated nor prolonged." Nevertheless, his function of intercession is prolonged: "The
anamnesis of Christ is the basis and source of all Christian prayer. So
our prayer relies upon and is united with the continual intercession of
the risen Lord."[23] What is new here is the description of the Eucharist
as the "sacrament" of the sacrifice of Christ, "the living and effective
sign" of his sacrifice. And sacrifice is here understood as encompassing

---

[21] A warning on this point was sounded for the Lutheran tradition in a report preparatory to the Lund Conference: "The Lutheran understanding of God's condescension
will have to guard against any separation of spiritual event and visible church action.
Worship will be deprived of its comforting strength, if it is so misunderstood that all
that happens in it is seen to represent merely the memorial of an event in the past.
This would interpose between the original event and the present congregation the
distance of history" (Herbert Goltzen, "The Elements of Worship," in *Ways of Worship*, eds. Pehr Edwall et al. [London, 1951], p. 97).
[22] *Baptism, Eucharist and Ministry*. Faith and Order Paper No. 111 (Geneva, 1982); history of the document, Preface, viii.
[23] *Ibid.*, the foregoing quotations from ##5, 8, & 9, pp. 11–12.

the total paschal mystery. What is puzzling is the seeming distinction especially between the resurrection and ascension of Christ, which as saving events cannot be "prolonged," and the high priestly intercession of Christ, which is "continual."

E vidence of a renewed interest in the sacrificial element of the Eucharist is provided also by theological works on the sacrament during this century. Keeping more closely to the traditions of this study, an examination of the contribution of some earlier representative Lutheran and Catholic theologians will be made.

Y ngve Brilioth lit the first spark of interest with his *Eucharistic Faith and Practice, Evangelical and Catholic*, first published in a Swedish edition in 1926.[24] As an early effort in ecumenism, this work pays special attention to the fact that Luther's thought leaves room in the sacrifice of Christ for some offering made by the participants. The highest offering they can make is that of themselves: incorporated into Christ by the sacrament, they offer themselves with Christ, sharing in his sacrifice. Brilioth believed that, with this idea of self-oblation, Luther was in contact with the highest conception of the eucharistic sacrifice of the early Church. Unfortunately, Luther never worked out this idea of sacrifice due to the "icy winds of controversy." The failure of Lutheran churches to recover the idea, either in liturgy or doctrine, has led, according to Brilioth, to their permanent impoverishment: "For the sacrificial idea lies so near to the heart of Christianity that it can never be neglected with impunity."[25]

S uch statements were bound to stimulate discussion on the sacrificial element in the Eucharist. The work of Gustaf Aulén, *Eucharist and Sacrifice*,[26] proved to be a similar catalyst. Besides drawing attention to the ideas of sacrifice that Luther regularly associated with the Eucharist—the sacrifices of praise, prayer and willing service—Aulén sees a distinct sacrificial emphasis in the serious affirmation of the Real Presence. The presence of the body and blood of Christ in the bread and wine is the presence of his sacrifice. What happens through the Real Presence is that the living Christ actualizes his eternally valid sacrifice and makes it into an effectively present reality. Hence, the sacrifice of Christ, although perfected in his death, is not merely something that

---

[24]   The English translation bearing this title was made by A. G. Hebert in 1930.
[25]   *Ibid.*, p. 138.
[26]   The English translation is by Eric H. Wahlstrom, 1958.

happened once in the past; it is a sacrifice that is valid for all time and for all generations.[27] This explanation of the sacrificial dimension of the Eucharist comes very close to any orthodox Catholic statement and, for that reason, goes far beyond, in my opinion, what Luther himself would have granted. Aulén's position here is interesting for the Catholic reader of Luther who finds a haunting enigma in the fact (as mentioned above, p. 101, n. 10) that the reformer did not draw precisely these same implications from his strong affirmation of the Real Presence, the presence of Christ *modo immolatitio* in Cajetan's phrase. Possibly the answer is that Luther's rejection of sacrifice in the Eucharist and his defence of the presence of Christ in the sacrament came at two different phases of his career, and he failed to see any real inconsistency in the two positions.[28]

To continue with a corollary of Aulén: since it is the presence of Christ that makes his sacrifice present in the Eucharist, the work of the sacrament is totally his work and due to no effort on our part. Consequently, any idea that we offer Christ is excluded by Aulén. Even this corollary could have a legitimate meaning within the Catholic tradition: Christ, as principal priest, offers his sacrifice to the Father in the Eucharist. Yet this same tradition would want to give some meaning to the expression "we offer Christ," especially in the sense that the sacrifice of Christ becomes also the sacrifice of his Body, which is the Church. Another Lutheran theologian, Regin Prenter, does not hesitate to justify use of this expression, claiming Luther himself as his authority. Its meaning, then, is the interpretation given it by the young Luther: that we, being united with Christ by the gift he has given us in the sacrament, ask him to represent us and to present our unworthy gifts to God in his name.[29] Luther *does* use the expression, and with approximately this meaning—a meaning, however, which comes out to be rather "we offer *with* Christ" than "we offer Christ."[30] Neverthe-

---

[27] *Ibid.*, p. 94.

[28] In Luther's earlier writings, the significance of Christ's body and blood in the Eucharist was that they constituted the sign of God's promise—an appropriate sign because they were the very means by which the inheritance of the promise, forgiveness of sin and eternal life, was secured. Cf. *Ein Sermon von dem neuen Testament, WA* 6, 358.

[29] Prenter, "Luther on Word and Sacrament," in *More About Luther*, 118.

[30] *Ein Sermon von dem neuen Testament, WA* 6, 371: ". . . durch wilchen (den Glauben) wir uns, unser nott, gepett, lob und danck auf Christo und durch Christo neben dem sacrament opffern, und damit Christum fur gott opffern, das ist, yhm ursach geben und bewegen, das er sich fur uns und uns mit yhm opffert."

less, such a meaning emphasizes the Christian's role as a member of the Body of Christ and is open to the acknowledgement of the Eucharist as the corporate offering of the Church. This aspect of worship, with roots in Luther himself, has perhaps not been fully appreciated in the Lutheran tradition.[31]

On the Catholic side, we could scarcely speak of a renewal of interest in the sacrificial element of the Eucharist in this century. The interest had always been there; but now it was expressed in theological works which benefitted by the more recent research into the nature of sacrifice. Early in the century, the thoroughness of such research was reflected in the comprehensive work of Maurice de la Taille, *Mysterium Fidei* (1921).[32] With an abundant use of patristic and scholastic sources, de la Taille treats, in turn, the sacrifice once offered by Christ himself, the Mass as the sacrifice of the Church, and the Eucharist as sacrament. His research safeguards the unity of Christ's sacrifice because there was only one real immolation: the ritual offering at the Last Supper looks forward to Christ's real immolation on Calvary; the ritual offering of the Mass by the Church looks back to the same oblation, deriving its efficacy from it.

Another work, representative of Catholic research in this century, is the study of Eugene Masure, *The Christian Sacrifice* (1944),[33] whose central thesis may be simply stated: the signs instituted by Christ contain and make real what they represent; the Eucharist was instituted by Christ as the sign of the sacrifice of the cross; therefore, the Eucharist contains and makes real the sacrifice of the cross.[34] In developing this thesis, Masure shows that the sacrifice of Christ includes more than his

---

[31]   Prenter, "Luther on Word and Sacrament," 118: "This genuinely Lutheran conception of the Eucharistic sacrifice has been forgotten in the Lutheran Church, and as a matter of fact, Luther did not himself emphasize it in his later writings. And that, I think, is a pity. For in the controversy with the Roman Catholic Church on this point, it has made us weaker than we needed to have been." Many Lutherans would not agree with Prenter. For example, Hermann Sasse, *This is My Body*, p. 21: "Nowhere in the New Testament do we find the idea of the Modern Liturgical Movement that the Church as the Body of Christ offers the sacrifice together with Christ, the Head." Cf. also Aulén, *Eucharist and Sacrifice*, pp. 97–98.

[32]   Translated into English by Joseph Carroll as *The Mystery of Faith*, Vol. I, 1940; Vol. II, 1950.

[33]   This is the title of the translation by Illtyd Trethowan.

[34]   Masure, *The Christian Sacrifice*, p. 15.

immolation on Calvary, important as this reality was to atone for human wickedness. Christ's sacrifice consists also in the return of the Son
to the Father with his attitude of love and obedience, and in the acceptance granted by the Father to this homage of the incarnate Son.
Although his sacrifice was *usque ad mortem, mortem autem crucis*, the
complete sacrificial action was *per passionem et crucem ad resurrectionis
gloriam*.[35] The Last Supper was a sign which received its full meaning
from Christ's sacrifice on Good Friday.[36] The Mass is an efficacious sign,
rich enough to make present the whole sacrifice of Christ, his oblation,
immolation and acceptance by the Father.[37] In celebrating the Mass,
the Church makes its own this unique sacrifice of Christ; the offering
of Christ becomes the offering of his Church.[38]

With the research of these and other theologians into the nature of
sacrifice and its relevance to the Eucharist, the way was prepared
in the second half of this century for theologians of both Lutheran and
Catholic traditions to enter into shared dialogue on the subject. In the
United States, participants in the dialogue presented and discussed
position papers on different aspects of the subject; the culmination was
a Statement, published in 1967. Papers, respective summaries of doctrine and the Statement are contained in *Lutherans and Catholics in Dialogue III: The Eucharist as Sacrifice*. The Statement contains points of
agreement: the Eucharist is a sacrifice, for in it Christ is present as the
Crucified who died for our sins and rose for our justification, as the
once-for-all sacrifice for the sins of the world who gives himself to the
faithful; the celebration of the Eucharist is the Church's sacrifice of
praise and self-offering.[39] The meaning of other points needs further
clarification: how the congregation "offers Christ"; how the eucharistic
sacrifice is "propitiatory"; how Mass intentions, stipends, and the mul-
tiplication of Masses are reconciled as practices with the all-sufficiency
of Christ's sacrifice.[40]

---

35 *Ibid.*, p. 185.
36 *Ibid.*, p. 239.
37 *Ibid.*, pp. 232, 265.
38 *Ibid.*, p. 218.
39 *Lutherans and Catholics in Dialogue* III, pp. 188–89.
40 *Ibid.*, pp. 189–91. The methodology of this Dialogue has been questioned by Kevin
    W. Irwin in *American Lutherans and Roman Catholics in Dialogue on the Eucharist: A
    Methodological Critique and Proposal* (Roma, 1979). Instead of a comparative study of

During the 1970s, an international Commission, established for ecumenical dialogue by the Vatican Secretariat for Christian Unity and the Lutheran World Federation, focused on the Eucharist and in 1978 issued the "Catholic–Lutheran Agreed Statement on the Eucharist."[41] In its formulation of areas of agreement and areas needing further research, it draws freely upon previous and current ecumenical Statements,[42] as well as advancing the common understanding of the two traditions. More comprehensive in its treatment of the Eucharist, it nevertheless deals in many places with the specific subject of this investigation. For example, concerning the meaning of memorial: "In the memorial celebration of the people of God, more happens than that past events are brought to mind by this power of recall and imagination. . . . In this creative act of God, the salvation event from the past becomes the offer of salvation for the present and the promise of salvation for the future."[43] On the once-for-all sacrifice of Christ: "This sacrifice can be neither continued, nor repeated, nor replaced, nor complemented; but rather it can and should become effective ever anew in the midst of the congregation."[44] On the fruits of the Mass, it offers some light on the query of the American dialogue mentioned above: "Christ's gift of his flesh and blood to those who receive the eucharist in faith cannot be transferred to others. Yet we may hope, however, that he allows others to share in his help. Whether or how this happens is entirely dependent on the sovereign love of the Lord. Intercessions

---

both traditions, Irwin strongly favours the present reformed liturgies of the traditions and specifically the eucharistic prayer as a more fruitful *locus theologicus* of the Dialogue. While the liturgical theology of this century can greatly assist and advance ecumenical dialogue, it cannot be considered apart from the eucharistic theology of the denominations and the common tradition of the Church. As the present study illustrates, one cannot fully appreciate the two liturgical treatises of Luther, *Formula Missae* and *Deutsche Messe* (Irwin, pp. 84–90), apart from his developing evangelical theology from 1512 onward and his eucharistic theology in other treatises.

[41] *Origins* VIII (January 11, 1979), 466–78.
[42] Especially the Statement of the American Lutheran–Catholic dialogue, the texts of agreement issued by the Commission of Faith and Order, as well as the Windsor Statement (1971) of the Anglican–Roman Catholic International Commission (ARCIC). The latter Statement and an Elucidation (1979) on it are contained in *The Final Report* of the ARCIC (London & Washington, 1982), pp. 12–25.
[43] "Catholic–Lutheran Agreed Statement" (*supra*, n. 41), #36, 471.
[44] *Ibid.*, #56, 473–74.

and intentions at the Mass for specific persons—living as well as dead—
do not limit his freedom."[45]

The description of the Eucharist as the continuing presence of the
unique sacrifice of Christ, the emphasis on participating in the Eucharist with praise and thanksgiving but also in a spirit of self-oblation,
the designation of the Eucharist as the offering of the Church—these
are indications, from both Lutheran and Catholic theologians and their
agreed Statements, of the growing acceptance in this century of some
sacrificial character of the Eucharist. Moreover, these aspects of the
sacrament have been discussed against the background of a broader
understanding of the nature of sacrifice than was possible in the sixteenth century. The present context is simply different from the context
of the age of the Reformation. In present-day discussions, we recognize
the development that has taken place between Luther and his interpreters today, as well as the parallel development between the Catholic
apologists and contemporary Catholic theologians. Further differences
in this aspect of the eucharistic doctrine will have to be discussed and
resolved in this present context.[46]

Is there any aspect of the sacrifice of Christ upon which further research
within the present context would lead to even closer agreement between the Lutheran and Catholic traditions concerning the sacrificial
character of the Eucharist? Further study of the nature of the heavenly
intercession of Christ would, I submit, achieve this end: if his work of
heavenly intercession could be accepted as an integral and essential part
of Christ's sacrifice, and if the Eucharist makes present the complete
sacrifice of Christ, then there are common grounds for accepting the
sacrificial character of the Eucharist.

The subject of Christ's heavenly intercession has not been entirely
overlooked by either Lutheran or Catholic traditions since the sixteenth century. Luther himself has a good description of it in his Commentary on Psalm 110 (1535). In the context, he is dealing precisely
with Christ's priestly office of intercession as it relates to his sacrifice:

> Undoubtedly this sacrifice, which He completed once for all the world's
> sins, suffices until the Last Day. But we are still sinful and spiritually

---

45 *Ibid.*, #61, 475.
46 Meinhold and Iserloh, *Abendmahl und Opfer*, pp. 85–86.

weak. Therefore He must unceasingly represent us before the Father and
intercede for us that such weakness and sin may not be reckoned to our
account. Rather He must grant us the strength and power of the Holy
Spirit to overcome sin. The reason why He ascended to heaven to sit at
the right hand of God was to preserve us forever in God's grace through
His intercessions and, further, to give us power and victory over the
terrors of sin, Satan, and the temptations of the world and our flesh (*WA*
41, 191; *LW* 13, 320).[47]

Although Christ's unique sacrifice is complete, his work of intercession
on behalf of sinners continues in his state of exaltation in heaven. Luther
would consider this work "priestly," but not "sacrificial," a term re-
served specifically for Christ's sacrifice whereby sinners are reconciled
to God. In a brief reference to intercession, alluding to Heb. 9:12, 24,
Cajetan likewise speaks of it as the work of Christ, the eternal Priest,
but, by using it as an analogy for Christ's activity in the Eucharist, he
would consider it also as sacrificial: "As Christ entered heaven by his
own blood to continue as an eternal priest interceding for us, so he
continues with us in the manner of an offering interceding for us in
the Eucharist."[48] Cajetan here speaks of three modes of Christ's intercession: the unique intercession of his death and, dependently related to this, his continual intercession in heaven, and his intercession
"in mystery" in the Eucharist.

Since the notion of sacrifice was limited in perspective during the
Reformation period to the passion and death of Christ, there was
little discussion of the eternal consequences of his saving work. As a
result, very few references to the heavenly intercession of Christ occur
in the writings of the Catholic apologists.[49] Still, within the Catholic

---

47 For other references in Luther, cf. *Ein Sermon von dem neuen Testament* (1520), *WA* 6,
    369; *Von der Freiheit eines Christenmenschen* (1520), *WA* 7, 56; *Deutsche Messe* (1526),
    WA 19, 99–100.

48 Cajetan, *De missae sacrificio, Opuscula Omnia*, t. III, tr. 10, p. 287; translation from
    Wicks, *Cajetan Responds*, p. 199.

49 Lepin, *L'Idée du sacrifice de la Messe*, pp. 277–78, mentions only Ruard Tapper and
    Lindanus, besides Cajetan, who treat the subject. David Power, *The Sacrifice We Offer*,
    pp. 76–79, adds Joannes Gropper and Franciscus Sonnius to Tapper as theologians
    who referred to Christ's heavenly intercession during the debates of the 1551–1552
    period of Trent: they spoke of one oblation of Christ, begun at the Last Supper, com-
    pleted on the cross, eternally enduring in heaven, and now sacramentally represented
    in the Mass. Bishop Julius von Pflug later voiced this same position but the connec-
    tion of these elements of Christ's one oblation, in hindsight so rich, was unfortu-
    nately not reflected in the doctrinal decrees of the Council (*ibid.*, pp. 86–87, 93).

tradition, a theoretical link with the broader notion of sacrifice was
maintained by the preservation of the Canon of the Mass which, as a
monument to the theology of the early Church, speaks of the eucharistic
action as a commemoration not only of the passion of Christ, but also
of his resurrection from the grave and of his ascension into heaven.[50]
In liturgical text, if not in theology, the elements for a richer conception of sacrifice were at hand, even though it was a long time before
the post-Tridentine Church made use of them. The same aid was not
available to the Lutheran tradition because Luther had eliminated the
Canon from its liturgy, except for the words of institution.[51]

Given the new context of sacrifice resulting from the research of the
nineteenth century, the heavenly intercession of Christ enters into
theological discussions more particularly in this century. The scriptural
basis of the discussions rests on the Epistle to the Hebrews, with attention to two specific texts: "Consequently, he [Christ] is able for all
time to save those who draw near to God through him, since he always
lives to make intercession for them" (7:25); and "For Christ has entered, not into a sanctuary made with hands, a copy of the true one,
but into heaven itself, now to appear in the presence of God on our
behalf" (9:24).

Lutheran theologians generally regard the heavenly intercession of
Christ as part of his function as High Priest, but hesitate to describe
it as "sacrificial," wishing to maintain a distinction between his act of
atonement and his intercessory activity. Thus Aulén, while using the
term "sacrifice" of both, distinguishes between Christ's atoning sacrifice and his intercessory sacrifice. The first is the perfect sacrifice in
his death made once for all, that sacrifice which is eternally valid and
eternally present, on the basis of which Christ is forever the heavenly
High Priest. The second is the continuous realization of the reconciliation which has been achieved in the atoning sacrifice; it is the intercession which the heavenly High Priest in solidarity with his Church

---

[50] The earliest text of the Eucharistic Prayer is contained in the *Traditio Apostolica* of
      Hippolytus of Rome and has been substantially preserved as Eucharistic Prayer II of
      the revised Roman Missal. Cf. Joseph Jungmann, *The Mass: An Historical, Theological
      and Pastoral Survey* (Collegeville, Minn., 1976), pp. 31–37.
[51] The potential for this principle of *lex orandi, lex credendi* at the time of the Reforma-
      tion is underlined, with regret, by Dix, *The Shape of the Liturgy*, pp. 625–26.

makes in order that the work of redemption may be realized on earth.[52] In a similar manner, Kent Knutson distinguishes the "state of humiliation" of Christ, including the events from the incarnation to his death, from the "state of exaltation," including those events by which God exalts his Son—the *descensus ad inferos*, resurrection and ascension. There is a continuity between the two states because it is the same Christ who died and rose again, who was born of Mary and sits at the right hand of the Father, the one who is both God and human forever. Yet there is also a radical discontinuity because the exalted Christ exists in a state of being which is no longer confined by space and time, which is no longer a state of suffering and shame, which is the beginning of an age that is a reign of victory and that occurred only after the completion of the acts of sacrifice in humiliation. Therefore, according to Knutson, the term "sacrifice," being especially related to Christ's death, applies more properly to his state of humiliation. Christ has both completed and continues his work, but he now continues his work in exaltation because he has completed his work in humiliation.[53] In the positions of both Knutson and Aulén, one can read a basic fidelity to Luther's own conception of heavenly intercession and its relation to the atoning act.

Max Thurian of the Community of Taizé, an ecumenical theologian in the Reformed tradition, would go a step further. Considering the yearly sacrifice of the Levitical high priest on the Day of Atonement—the constant frame of reference for the sacrifice of Christ in Hebrews—Thurian observes that this rite of expiation was performed in two stages: first, the sacrifice for sin on the altar, then the aspersion with blood in the sanctuary, beyond the veil, on the throne of mercy. The author of Hebrews saw in this rite the symbol of the two stages of Christ's expiation: first, the sacrifice for sin on the altar of the cross, then the entrance into the heavenly sanctuary with the blood of sacrifice as his perpetual intercession. Hence, according to Thurian's interpretation, there are not two "works" of Christ involved here, but the twofold aspect of his one and unique sacrifice for the forgiveness of

---

[52]   Cf. Aulén, *Eucharist and Sacrifice*, pp. 152–53 and, more briefly, his summary, p. 167.

[53]   Kent Knutson, "Contemporary Lutheran Theology and the Eucharistic Sacrifice," in *Lutherans and Catholics in Dialogue* III, p. 176.

sins, historical and perpetual, once and for all and unceasingly. The sacrificial character of the Eucharist is connected with both the sacrifice of Christ on the cross and his entrance as High Priest into the sanctuary of heaven, beyond the veil, bearing the blood of his sacrifice as a perpetual intercession.[54]

Using the same context for the offering of the Eucharist, and profiting from further research on the notion of memorial, Thurian has more recently expressed his position this way:

> If we return to what the Jewish liturgy of the Passover meal provides for the understanding of the Eucharist in depth, we might offer the following summary to explain why it can be said that the Eucharist is a sacrifice:
>
> 1. it is a *sacrifice of praise and thanksgiving* recalling the marvels wrought by God in the order of creation and the order of redemption;
> 2. it is the *sacrament of the unique sacrifice* of Christ: the sacramental presence of the sacrifice of the cross;
> 3. it is the *liturgical presentation* of the sacrifice of the Son by the Church to the Father, to remind him of this people and to grant them the blessings afforded by that unique sacrifice;
> 4. it is *participation in the Son's intercession* with the Father for the gift of salvation to all people and for the coming of the kingdom of God.[55]

This summary by Thurian of Christ's heavenly intercession linking the unique sacrifice of Christ and the celebration of the Eucharist comes very close to the understanding expressed by some Catholic theologians, especially by Catholic exegetes and commentators on Hebrews. In a significant article some years ago,[56] Stanislaus Lyonnet

---

[54] Thurian, *The One Bread*, p. 30. A similar view of the heavenly intercession of Christ within the total act of the atonement is presented by an Anglican, E. O. James, in his *Sacrifice and Sacrament* (London, 1962), pp. 127–28.

[55] *The Mystery of the Eucharist: An Ecumenical Approach*, trans. Emily Chisholm (London & Oxford, 1983), pp. 19–20; emphasis in original. This work reflects the terminology and perspective of the Lima document, *Baptism, Eucharist and Ministry*, and not surprisingly, since Thurian is acknowledged as the "major architect" of its text; cf. Michael A. Fahey, S.J., "Consensus on the Eucharist," *The Month* N.S. XVIII (October 1985), 337. One may note the development of Thurian's thought, remaining faithful nevertheless to the idea of a single offering of Christ under different aspects, by comparing the above quotation with a summary statement in his earlier work, *The Eucharistic Memorial*. Part II *The New Testament*, trans. J. G. Davies (Richmond, Va., 1961), p. 13.

[56] "Expiation et Intercession," *Biblica* XL (September 1959), 885–901.

sought to throw some light on the biblical meaning of "intercession" (*entunchanein*). He pointed out that in some books of the Old Testament, for example, Exodus (32:11ff.; 32:30) and Numbers (16:44–48, together with Wisdom 18:21–25), and in the Targum material, St. Jerome in the Vulgate regularly translates the Hebrew verb for "to make expiation" by the Latin verb "to pray" or "to intercede": *rogare, deprecari.*[57] Hence, to make expiation can bear the meaning: to intercede on behalf of someone by means of prayers. This assimilation of meaning may also be understood by the author of Hebrews who, in describing Christ's entry into the heavenly sanctuary, speaks of the performance of his sacerdotal function as "intercession," having in mind the entry of the Levitical high priest into the Holy of Holies, there to complete the expiatory rite by sprinkling the sacrificial blood on the propitiatory.[58] If *entunchanein* bears this meaning in Heb. 7:25, then as Myles Bourke concludes, "the intercession of the Exalted Christ should not be regarded as the sequel to his sacrifice, but as its eternal continuance in heaven."[59]

In stressing the sacrificial character of the heavenly intercession and, by implication, the sacrificial character of the Eucharist as associated with it, a danger must be avoided: that of viewing the sacrifice of the Eucharist as setting forth only the present intercessory activity of Christ, the High Priest. To do so would be as limited as to regard the sacrifice of the Eucharist as re-presenting only an earthly event, as restricted to the sacrifice on Calvary. A balance must be maintained. The sacrifice of the Eucharist must re-present the whole sacrifice of Christ, the one sacrifice which, after the paradigm of the Day of Atone-

[57] *Ibid.*, 885–92; also in *Sin, Redemption and Sacrifice. A Biblical and Patristic Study* by Lyonnet and Léopold Sabourin (Rome, 1970), pp. 141–48.

[58] Lyonnet, "Expiation et Intercession," 897–98.

[59] Myles M. Bourke, *The Epistle to the Hebrews* in *The Jerome Biblical Commentary*, p. 394, #42. This perspective on the complete sacrifice of Christ speaks to the concern of the Vatican in its recent official response to the Lima document (*Baptism, Eucharist and Ministry*) as to whether the continuity of Christ's saving work is adequately described by "intercession"; cf. "Baptism, Eucharist and Ministry: An Appraisal" in *Origins* XVII (November 19, 1987), 401–16, and specifically 409–10. For the continuing interpretation of Hebrews 7:25, cf. David Peterson, *Hebrews and Perfection. An Examination of the Concept of Perfection in the 'Epistle to the Hebrews'* (Cambridge/London, 1982), pp. 113–16, and especially p. 248, n. 64, for the interpretation of Christ's "intercession" in the different Christian traditions.

ment sacrifice, began on earth and reaches completion in heaven.[60]
Constant attention to the dominant image of Christ in the Book of
Revelation as the Lamb once slain who lives forever would help to
maintain this balance.[61]

The foregoing presentation of the views of contemporary theologians
concerning the heavenly intercession of Christ has revealed some
points of difference and some areas of agreement between the two traditions which have been the principal focus of this study. Further research on the meaning of this aspect of Christ's atoning work and its
implication for the nature of the Eucharist could only benefit both
churches. For Lutherans, the discussion would be clearly removed from
the "sacrifice = death" emphasis: after centuries, there is still the
lingering misapprehension that the death of Christ is repeated in each
sacrifice of the Mass! For Catholics, the discussion would favour a theory
of sacrifice adopted and set forth by several theologians,[62] which com-
bines as constitutive elements the interior sacrificial attitude of Christ
with an appropriate and efficacious symbol. This balance of emphasis
on the subjective–objective elements of sacrifice, rather than on the
purely objective as heretofore, might prove more congenial to Lutheran
theologians. As research and discussion proceed, other benefits would
undoubtedly emerge. The points of difference would diminish, the
areas of agreement increase. Perhaps one day, with a greater measure
of doctrinal understanding, with participation from the same table,
the Eucharist may in fact become what it was meant to be—the sacrament of unity among Christians.

---

[60]   Cf. Bourke, *The Epistle to the Hebrews*, p. 398, #53, for his comment on Heb. 9:14
       (". . . who through the eternal spirit offered himself . . ."): "This verse is another
       statement that Jesus's self-offering is a heavenly, not an earthly reality, since it is of-
       fered through the eternal spirit, i.e. in that new sphere of existence that he enters at
       the time of his exaltation. Clearly, the author does not question the importance of the
       cross, nor does he mean that the sacrifice lies wholly in the heavenly sphere, but only
       that the sacrifice is consummated there."
[61]   The need for such balance is maintained by other authors: Thurian, *The Eucharistic
       Memorial*, Part II, p. 82; Averbeck, *Der Opfercharakter des Abendmahls*, pp. 803–804;
       Hay, "Theology of Eucharist: The Church's Spiritual Sacrifice," 16–17, 20; and
       David M. Stanley, "Ecumenically Significant Aspects of New Testament Eucharistic
       Doctrine," *Concilium*, Vol. XXIV (New York, 1966), 49.
[62]   For example: Masure, *The Christian Sacrifice*, pp. 263–64; Rahner and Häussling, *The
       Celebration of the Eucharist*, pp. 16–17; Bernard Lonergan, *De notione sacrificii*
       (Toronto, 1960), p. 1.

BIBLIOGRAPHY

SOURCES

Anselm of Canterbury, St. *Cur Deus Homo? Basic Writings*. Translated by S. N. Deane. LaSalle, Ill., 1962.

Aquinas, St. Thomas. *Summa Theologica*. Turin, 1928.

Biel, Gabriel. *Gabrielis Biel Canonis Misse Expositio*. Edited by Heiko Oberman and William Courtenay. Wiesbaden, 1963–1967.

Cajetan, Cardinal. *Opuscula Omnia*. Venice, 1588. Containing:
—*De missae celebratione* (1509–1510).
—*De erroribus contingentibus in eucharistiae sacramento* (1525).
—*De missae sacrificio et ritu adversus Lutheranos* (1531).

Contarini, Gaspar. *Confutatio articulorum seu quaestionum Lutheranorum* (1530). *Corpus Catholicorum*, Vol. VII. Münster, 1923.

Eck, Johannes. *De sacrificio missae libri tres* (1526). Edited by Erwin Iserloh, Vinzenz Pfnür and Peter Fabisch. *Corpus Catholicorum*, Vol. XXXVI. Münster, 1982.

Emser, Jerome. *Corpus Catholicorum*, Vol. XXVIII. Münster, 1959. Containing:
—*Missae Christianorum contra Lutheranam missandi formulam assertio* (1524).
—*Auff Luthers grewel wider die heiligen Stillmess Antwort* (1525).

Fisher, John. *Sacri Sacerdotii Defensio contra Lutherum* (1525). *Corpus Catholicorum*, Vol. IX. Münster, 1925.

Henry VIII. *Assertio Septem Sacramentorum* (1521). Edited by Louis O'Donovan. New York, 1908.

Luther, Martin. *D. Martin Luthers Werke, Krit. Gesamtausgabe*. Weimar, 1883–. Containing:
—*D.M.L. Commentariolus in epistolam divi Pauli Apostoli ad Hebraeos* (1517).
—*Ein Sermon von dem hochwürdigen Sakrament des heiligen wahren Leichnams Christi und von den Brüderschaften* (1519).
—*Von den guten Werken* (1520).
—*Ein Sermon von dem neuen Testament, das ist von der heiligen Messe* (1520).
—*De captivitate Babylonica ecclesiae praeludium* (1520).

—*Vom Missbrauch der Messe* (1521).

—*Contra Henricum Regem Angliae* (1522).

—*Von Ordnung Gottesdiensts in der Gemeine* (1523).

—*Von Anbeten des Sakraments des heiligen Leichnams Christi* (1523).

—*Formula Missae et Communionis* (1523).

—*De instituendis ministris Ecclesiae* (1524).

—*Vom Greuel der Stillmesse* (1525).

—*Deutsche Messe und Ordnung Gottesdiensts* (1526).

—*Dass diese Wort Christi "Das ist mein Leib" noch fest stehen wider die Schwarmgeister* (1527).

—*Vom Abendmahl Christi, Bekenntnis* (1528).

—*Vermahnung an die Geistlichen, versammelt auf dem Reichstag zu Augsburg. Anno 1530.*

—*Vermahnung zum Sakrament des Leibes und Blutes Christi* (1530).

—*Von der Winkelmesse und Pfaffenweihe* (1533).

—*Der CX Psalm, Gepredigt und ausgelegt durch D. Mart. Luth.* (1535).

—*Die Disputation contra missam privatam* (1536).

—*Die Schmalkaldischen Artikel* (1537–1538).

—*Kurzes Bekenntnis vom heiligen Sacrament* (1544).

———. *D. Martin Luthers Werke, Krit. Gesamtausgabe. Briefe.* Weimar, 1930–.

———. *D. Martin Luthers Werke, Krit. Gesamtausgabe. Tischreden.* Weimar, 1912.

Peter the Venerable. *Tractatus contra Petrobrusianos. Patrologia Latina.* Edited by J. P. Migne. Vol. CLXXXIX. Paris, 1844–.

Radbertus, Paschasius. *De Corpore et Sanguine Domini. Patrologia Latina.* Edited by J. P. Migne. Vol. CXX. Paris, 1844–.

Schatzgeyer, Kaspar. *Schriften zur Verteidigung der Messe.* Edited, with introductions, by Erwin Iserloh and Peter Fabisch. *Corpus Catholicorum,* Vol. XXXVII. Münster, 1984.

LITERATURE

Althaus, Paul. *The Theology of Martin Luther.* Translated by Robert C. Schultz. Philadelphia: Fortress Press, 1966.

Anglican–Roman Catholic International Commission. *The Final Report.* Edited by H. R. McAdoo and Alan C. Clark. London: SPCK/Washington: U.S. Catholic Conference, 1982.

Atkinson, James. *The Trial of Luther.* New York: Stein & Day, 1971.

———. *Martin Luther and the Birth of Protestantism.* Atlanta, Ga.: John Knox Press, 1981[2].

Aulén, Gustaf. *Christus Victor.* Translated by A. G. Hebert. London: Society for Promoting Christian Knowledge, 1950[6].

————. *Eucharist and Sacrifice*. Translated by Eric H. Wahlstrom. Philadelphia: Muhlenberg Press, 1958.

Averbeck, Wilhelm. *Der Opfercharakter des Abendmahls in der neueren evangelischen Theologie*. Paderborn: Verlag Bonifacius, 1966.

Bainton, Roland. *Here I Stand: A Life of Martin Luther*. Mentor Books. New York: The New American Library, 1950.

Baptism, Eucharist and Ministry. Faith and Order Paper No. 111 of the World Council of Churches (WCC). Geneva, 1982.

"Baptism, Eucharist and Ministry: An Appraisal." Vatican Response to WCC Document. *Origins* XVII (November 19, 1987), 401–16.

Boehmer, Heinrich. *Road to Reformation*. Translated by John W. Doberstein and Theodore G. Tappert. Philadelphia: Muhlenberg Press, 1946.

Bourke, Myles M. *The Epistle to the Hebrews. The Jerome Biblical Commentary*. Edited by Raymond E. Brown et al. Englewood Cliffs, N.J.: Prentice-Hall, 1968.

Brecht, Martin. *Martin Luther*: Bd. 1 *Sein Weg zur Reformation, 1483–1521*. Stuttgart: Calwer Verlag, 1981. Bd. 2 *Ordnung und Abgrenzung der Reformation, 1521–1532* (1986). Bd. 3 *Die Erhaltung der Kirche, 1532–1546* (1987). Bd. 1 translated by James L. Schaaf, *Martin Luther: His Road to Reformation, 1483–1521*. Philadelphia: Fortress Press, 1985.

Brilioth, Yngve. *Eucharistic Faith and Practice, Evangelical and Catholic*. Translated by A. G. Hebert. London: Society for Promoting Christian Knowledge, 1953[3].

Burgess, Joseph A., ed. *The Role of the Augsburg Confession: Catholic and Lutheran Views*. Philadelphia: Fortress Press, 1980.

Cargill-Thompson, W.D.J. "The Problem of Luther's 'Tower Experience' and Its Place in his Intellectual Development," in *Studies in the Reformation: Luther to Hooker*. Edited by C. W. Dugmore. London: The Athlone Press, 1980, 60–80.

"Catholic–Lutheran Agreed Statement on the Eucharist," *Origins* VIII (January 11, 1979), 466–78.

Clark, Francis. *Eucharistic Sacrifice and the Reformation*. London: Darton, Longman & Todd, 1960[2].

Congar, Yves. *Vraie et fausse réforme dans l'Eglise. Unam Sanctam*, #20. Paris: Editions du Cerf, 1950.

Daly, Robert J. *Christian Sacrifice: The Judaeo-Christian Background before Origen*. Washington: Catholic University of America Press, 1978.

Dix, Dom Gregory. *The Shape of the Liturgy*. London: Dacre Press, 1970[10].

Doernberg, Erwin. *Henry VIII and Luther*. London: Baine & Rockliff, 1961.

Dolan, John P. *History of the Reformation. A Conciliatory Assessment of Opposite Views*. New York: Desclée Co., 1965.

Edwards, Mark U., Jr. *Luther and the False Brethren*. Stanford: Stanford University Press, 1975.

Fahey, Michael A., S.J. "Consensus on the Eucharist," *The Month* N.S. XVIII (October 1985), 334–40.

Feld, Helmut. *Das Verständnis des Abendmahls.* Darmstadt: Wissenschaftliche Buchgesellschaft, 1976.

Fitzmyer, Joseph A. *The Letter to the Galatians. The Jerome Biblical Commentary.* Edited by Raymond E. Brown et al. Englewood Cliffs, N.J.: Prentice-Hall, 1968.

Franks, R. S. *The Work of Christ.* London: Nelson, 1962.

Franz, Adolph. *Die Messe im deutschen Mittelalter.* Freiburg im Bresgau: Herder, 1902.

Gaudel, A. "L'Idée catholique de la Messe à la Veille de la Réforme," *Dictionnaire de Théologie Catholique*, Vol. X, 1. Edited by A. Vacant et al. Paris, 1928. Cols. 1081–84.

Gerrish, Brian. "Priesthood and Ministry in the Theology of Luther," *Church History* XXXIV (December 1965), 404–22.

Goltzen, Herbert. "The Elements of Worship," in *Ways of Worship.* Edited by Pehr Edwall et al. London: SCM Press, 1951.

Graebke, Friedrich. *Die Konstruction der Abendmahlslehre Luthers in ihrer Entwicklung dargestellt.* Leipzig: A. Deichert, 1908.

Grass, H. *Die Abendmahlslehre bei Luther und Calvin: Eine kritische Untersuchung.* Gütersloh: C. Bertelsmann Verlag, 1954.

Grisar, Hartmann. *Luther.* Vol. I. Translated by E. M. Lamond. London: B. Herder, 1913.

Haendler, Gert. *Luther on Ministerial Office and Congregational Function.* Translated by Ruth C. Gritch, edited by Eric W. Gritch. Philadelphia: Fortress Press, 1981.

Hagen, Kenneth G. "Changes in the Understanding of Luther: The Development of the Young Luther," *Theological Studies* XXIX (September 1968), 672–93.

————. *A Theology of Testament in the Young Luther. The Lectures on Hebrews.* Leiden: E. J. Brill, 1974.

Haile, H. G. *Luther: An Experiment in Biography.* New York: Doubleday, 1980.

Harran, Marilyn J. *Luther on Conversion: The Early Years.* Ithaca, N.Y.: Cornell University Press, 1983.

Häussling, Angelus. "Ursprünge der Privatmesse," *Stimmen der Zeit* CLXXVI (April 1965), 21–28.

Hay, David W. "Theology of Eucharist: The Church's Spiritual Sacrifice," *National Bulletin on Liturgy*, Vol. XV, No. 82 (January–February 1982), 11–22.

Hendrix, Scott H. *Luther and the Papacy: Stages in a Reformation Conflict.* Philadelphia: Fortress Press, 1981.

Heron, Alasdair I. C. *Table and Tradition. Toward an Ecumenical Understanding of the Eucharist.* Philadelphia: Westminster Press, 1983.

Hicks, F.C.N. *The Fullness of Sacrifice.* London: Macmillan, 1953[3].

Hillerbrand, Hans J. *The Reformation: A Narrative History Related by Contemporary Observers and Participants.* New York: Harper & Row, 1964.

Hodgson, Leonard, ed. *The Second World Conference on Faith and Order*. Edinburgh, 1937. New York: Macmillan, 1938.

Horvath, Tibor. *The Sacrificial Interpretation of Jesus' Achievement in the New Testament*. New York: Philosophical Library, 1979.

Hughes, John Jay. *Stewards of the Lord: A Reappraisal of Anglican Orders*. London: Sheed & Ward, 1970.

Irwin, Kevin W. *American Lutherans and Roman Catholics in Dialogue on the Eucharist: A Methodological Critique and Proposal*. Studia Anselmiana, #76. Roma: Editrice Anselmiana, 1979.

Iserloh, Erwin. *Die Eucharistie in der Darstellung des Johannes Eck. Reformations-geschichtliche Studien und Texte*, Heft 73/74. Münster: Aschendorff, 1950.

————. *Der Kampf um die Messe in den ersten Jahren der Auseinandersetzung mit Luther. Katholisches Leben und Kämpfen im Zeitalter der Glaubensspaltung*, #10. Münster: Aschendorff, 1952.

————. *Luther zwischen Reform und Reformation. Der Thesenanschlag fand nicht statt*. Münster: Aschendorff, 1968[3].

————. "Luther and the Council of Trent," *Catholic Historical Review* LXIX (October 1983), 563–76.

James, E. O. *Sacrifice and Sacrament*. London: Thames & Hudson, 1962.

Jedin, Hubert. *A History of the Council of Trent*, Vol. II. Translated by Ernest Graf. St. Louis: B. Herder, 1957.

Jensen, DeLamar. *Confrontation at Worms. Martin Luther and the Diet of Worms*. Provo, Utah: Brigham Young University Press, 1973.

Jungmann, Joseph. *The Mass of the Roman Rite: Its Origins and Development*, Vol. I. Translated by Francis E. Brunner. New York: Benzinger, 1950.

————. "Liturgy on the Eve of the Reformation," *Worship* XXXIII (August–September 1959), 505–15.

————. *The Mass: An Historical, Theological and Pastoral Survey*. Collegeville, Minn.: The Liturgical Press, 1976.

Kidd, B. J. *The Later Medieval Doctrine of the Eucharistic Sacrifice*. London: Society for Promoting Christian Knowledge, 1958.

La Taille, Maurice de. *The Mystery of Faith*. 2 vols. Translated by Joseph Carroll. New York: Sheed & Ward, 1940, 1950.

Leaver, Robin A. *Luther on Justification*. St. Louis: Concordia Publishing House, 1975.

Lehmann, Karl and Edmund Schlink, eds. *Das Opfer Jesu Christi und seine Gegenwart in der Kirche: Klärungen zum Opfercharakter des Herrenmahles*. Freiburg i. Br.: Herder, 1983.

Lepin, M. *L'Idée du sacrifice de la Messe d'après les Théologiens depuis l'origine jusqu'à nos jours*. Paris: Gabriel Beauchesne, 1926.

Lieberg, Hellmut. *Amt und Ordination bei Luther und Melanchthon*. Göttingen: Vandenhoeck & Ruprecht, 1962.

Lindberg, Carter. "Prierias and His Significance for Luther's Development," *The Six-teenth Century Journal* III (October 1972), 45–64.

———. "Luther's Views on Papal Authority," *Andover Newton Quarterly* XVII (Number 3, 1977), 213–26.

Lonergan, Bernard. *De notione sacrificii*. Unpublished manuscript. Regis College, Toronto, 1960. 18pp.

———. *De Verbo Incarnato*. Rome: Gregorian University Press, 1964[3].

Lortz, Joseph. *The Reformation in Germany*. 2 vols. Translated by Ronald Walls. New York: Herder & Herder, 1968.

Lyonnet, Stanislaus. "Expiation et Intercession," *Biblica* XL (September 1959), 885–901.

——— and Léopold Sabourin. *Sin, Redemption and Sacrifice. A Biblical and Patristic Study. Analecta Biblica*, #48. Rome: Biblical Institute Press, 1970.

Maly, Eugene H. *Genesis. The Jerome Biblical Commentary*. Edited by Raymond E. Brown et al. Englewood Cliffs, N.J.: Prentice-Hall, 1968.

Mann, Frido. *Das Abendmahl beim jungen Luther. Beiträge zur ökumenischen Theologie*. Bd. 5. Munich: Max Hüber Verlag, 1971.

Manns, Peter. "Amt und Eucharistie in der Theologie Martin Luthers," in Peter Bläser, *Amt und Eucharistie*. Paderborn: Bonifacius-Druckerei, 1973, 68–173.

Mascall, E. L. *Corpus Christi: Essays on the Church and on the Eucharist*. London: Longmans, Green & Co. Ltd., 1960[4].

Masure, Eugene. *The Christian Sacrifice*. Translated by Illtyd Trethowan. London: Burns, Oates & Washbourne, 1944.

McDonough, Thomas M. *The Law and the Gospel in Luther: A Study of Martin Luther's Confessional Writings*. Oxford: Oxford University Press, 1963.

McNally, Robert E. *The Reform of the Church: Crisis and Criticism in Historical Perspective*. New York: Herder & Herder, 1963.

———. *The Unreformed Church*. New York: Sheed & Ward, 1965.

———. "The Ninety-Five Theses of Martin Luther: 1517–1967," *Theological Studies* XXVIII (September 1967), 439–80.

Meinhold, Peter and Erwin Iserloh. *Abendmahl und Opfer*. Stuttgart: Schwabenverlag, 1966.

Meyer, Hans Bernhard. *Luther und die Messe*. Paderborn: Verlag Bonifacius, 1965.

Moll, Helmut. *Die Lehre von der Eucharistie als Opfer*. Köln: Peter Hanstein Verlag, 1975.

"Mysterium Fidei." Encyclical of Pope Paul VI. *Acta Apostolicae Sedis* LVII (October 1965), 753–74.

Nussbaum, Otto. *Kloster, Priestermönch und Privatmesse*. Bonn: Peter Hanstein Verlag, 1961.

Oberman, Heiko. *Forerunners of the Reformation*. New York: Holt, Rinehart & Winston, 1966.

————. *The Harvest of Medieval Theology*. Grand Rapids, Mich.: William B. Eerdmans, 1967.

————. "Headwaters of the Reformation: Initia Lutheri—Initia Reformationis," in *Luther and the Dawn of the Modern Era*. Edited by H. Oberman. Leiden: E. J. Brill, 1974, 40–88.

Olivier, Daniel. *The Trial of Luther*. Translated by John Tonkin. London/Oxford: Mobrays, 1978.

Ozment, Steven. "Luther and the Middle Ages: The Formation of Reformation Thought," in *Transition and Revolution*. Edited by Robert Kingdon. Minneapolis: Burgess Press, 1974, 109–52.

————. *The Age of Reform, 1250–1550. An Intellectual and Religious History of Late Medieval and Reformation Europe*. New Haven: Yale University Press, 1980.

————, ed. *Reformation Europe: A Guide to Research*. St. Louis: Center for Reformation Research, 1982.

Padberg, Rudolf. "Luther und der Canon Missae," *Catholica* XXXVII (No. 4, 1983), 288–305.

Pelikan, Jaroslav. "Luther and the Liturgy," in *More About Luther*. Vol. II. Martin Luther Lectures. Decorah, Iowa: Luther College Press, 1958, 3–62.

————. *Luther the Expositor: Introduction to the Reformer's Exegetical Writings*. St. Louis: Concordia Publishing House, 1959.

————. "The Theology of the Means of Grace," in *Accents in Luther's Theology: Essays in Commemoration of the 450th Anniversary of the Reformation*. Edited by H. Kadai. St. Louis: Concordia Publishing House, 1967, 124–47.

Pesch, Otto Hermann. *Hinführung zu Luther*. Mainz: Matthias-Grünewald, 1982.

Peterson, David. *Hebrews and Perfection. An Examination of the Concept of Perfection in the 'Epistle to the Hebrews.'* Cambridge/London: Cambridge University Press, 1982.

Power, David N. *The Sacrifice We Offer. The Tridentine Dogma and Its Reinterpretation*. New York: Crossroad Publishing, 1987.

Powers, Joseph M. *Eucharistic Theology*. New York: Herder & Herder, 1967.

Pratzner, Ferdinand. *Messe und Kreuzesopfer. Die Krise der sakramentalen Idee bei Luther und in der mittelalterlichen Scholastik*. Wien: Verlag Herder, 1970.

Prenter, Regin. *Spiritus Creator*. Translated by John M. Jensen. Philadelphia: Muhlenberg Press, 1953.

————. "Luther on Word and Sacrament," in *More About Luther*. Vol. II. Martin Luther Lectures. Decorah, Iowa: Luther College Press, 1958, 65–122.

Quere, Ralph W. "Changes and Constants: Structure in Luther's Understanding of the Real Presence in the 1520's," *The Sixteenth Century Journal* XVI (Spring 1985), 45–76.

Rahner, Karl and Angelus Häussling. *The Celebration of the Eucharist*. Translated by W. J. O'Hara. New York: Herder & Herder, 1968.

Reed, Luther D. *The Lutheran Liturgy*. Revised ed. Philadelphia: Muhlenberg Press, 1959.

Richard, Louis. *The Mystery of the Redemption*. Baltimore, Md.: Helicon Press, 1965.

Rodger, P. C. and Lucas Fischer, eds. *The Fourth World Conference on Faith and Order*. Montreal, 1963. New York: Association Press, 1964.

Rupp, Gordon. *Luther's Progress to the Diet of Worms*. Harper Torchbooks. New York: Harper & Row, 1964.

Sasse, Hermann. *This Is My Body*. Minneapolis: Augsburg Publishing House, 1959.

Schneider, Theodor. "Opfer Jesu Christi und der Kirche: zum Verständnis der Aussagen des Konzils von Trient," *Catholica* XXXI (1977), 51–65.

Schroeder, H. J., trans. *Canons and Decrees of the Council of Trent*. St. Louis: B. Herder, 1960[4].

Schwab, Wolfgang. *Entwicklung und Gestalt der Sakramententheologie bei Martin Luther*. Frankfurt: Verlag Peter Lang, 1977.

Schwiebert, E. G. *Luther and His Times*. St. Louis: Concordia Publishing House, 1950.

Seeberg, Reinhold. *Lehrbuch der Dogmengeschichte*. Vol. IV, 1. Graz: Akademische Verlaganstalt, 1953[5].

Sheedy, Charles E. *The Eucharistic Controversy of the Eleventh Century*. Washington: Catholic University Press, 1947.

Sider, Ronald J. *Andreas Bodenstein von Karlstadt*. Leiden: E. J. Brill, 1974.

———, ed. *Karlstadt's Battle with Luther: Documents in a Liberal–Radical Debate*. Philadelphia: Fortress Press, 1978.

Siggins, Ian. *Martin Luther's Doctrine of Christ*. Publications in Religion, #14. New Haven, Conn.: Yale University Press, 1970.

———. *Luther and His Mother*. Philadelphia: Fortress Press, 1981.

Stanley, David M. "Ecumenically Significant Aspects of New Testament Eucharistic Doctrine," *Concilium*, Vol. XXIV (New York: Paulist Press, 1966), 43–50.

Stevenson, Kenneth W. *Eucharist and Offering*. New York: Pueblo Publishing, 1986.

Tentler, Thomas N. *Sin and Confession on the Eve of the Reformation*. Princeton: Princeton University Press, 1977.

Theisen, Reinhold. *Mass Liturgy and the Council of Trent*. Collegeville, Minn.: St. John's University Press, 1965.

Thurian, Max. *The Eucharistic Memorial*. Part II *The New Testament*. Translated by J. G. Davies. Richmond, Va.: John Knox Press, 1961.

———. *The One Bread*. Translated by Theodore DuBois. New York: Sheed & Ward, 1969.

———. *The Mystery of the Eucharist: An Ecumenical Approach*. Translated by Emily Chisholm. London/Oxford: Mobrays, 1983.

Todd, John M. *Luther: A Life*. New York: Crossroads, 1982.

Tomkins, Oliver S., ed. *The Third World Conference on Faith and Order*. Lund, 1952. London: SCM Press, 1953.

Urban, P. Linwood, Jr. *The Will of God: A Study of the Origin and Development of Nominalism and Its Influence upon the Reformation*. Unpublished Ph.D. dissertation. General Theological Seminary, New York, 1959.

U.S.A. National Committee of the Lutheran World Federation and the Bishops' Commission for Ecumenical Affairs, Washington, D.C. Joint Publications:
—*Lutherans and Catholics in Dialogue* III: *The Eucharist as Sacrifice* (1967).
—*Lutherans and Catholics in Dialogue* IV: *Eucharist and Ministry* (1970).

Vajta, Vilmos. *Luther on Worship*. Translated by U. S. Leupold. Philadelphia: Fortress Press, 1958.

Van de Pol, W. H. *The Christian Dilemma*. Translated by G. Van Hall. London: J. M. Kent, 1952.

Wicks, Jared. *Man Yearning for Grace*. Washington/Cleveland: Corpus Books, 1968.
———. *Cajetan Responds: A Reader in Reformation Controversy*. Washington, D.C.: Catholic University of America Press, 1978.
———. "Abuses Under Indictment at Augsburg," *Theological Studies* XLI (June 1980), 253–302.
———. *Cajetan und die Anfänge der Reformation*. Translated from English by Barbara Hallensleben. Münster: Aschendorff, 1983.
———. "Justification and Faith in Luther," *Theological Studies* XLIV (March 1983), 3–29.
———. *Luther and His Spiritual Legacy*. Wilmington, Del.: Michael Glazier, 1983.
———. "Roman Reactions to Luther: The First Year (1518)," *Catholic Historical Review* LIX (October 1983), 521–62.
———. "Fides sacramenti—Fides specialis: Luther's Development in 1518," *Gregorianum* LXV (Fasc. #1, 1984), 53–87.

Wisløff, Carl F. *The Gift of Communion*. Translated by Joseph M. Shaw. Minneapolis: Augsburg Publishing House, 1964.

REFERENCES

Book of Concord. Translated and edited by Theodore G. Tappert. Philadelphia, 1959.
Dictionnaire de Théologie Catholique. Edited by A. Vacant et al. Paris, 1928.
Enchiridion Symbolorum. 34th ed. Edited by Henricus Denzinger and Adolphus Schönmetzer. Rome, 1966.
Lexikon für Theologie und Kirche. Edited by Josef Höfer and Karl Rahner. Freiburg, 1957–1965.
New Catholic Encyclopedia. Edited by Most Rev. William J. McDonald et al. New York, 1967.

Oxford Dictionary of the Christian Church, The. 2nd ed. Edited by F. L. Cross and E. A. Livingstone. London, 1974.

Vatican Council II: The Conciliar and Post Conciliar Documents. Edited by Austin Flannery. Collegeville, Minn., 1975.

INDEX